NO MORE JUNK FOOD

WENDY MCCALLUM, RHN

D1476794

FORMAC PUBLISHING COMPANY LIMITED
HALIFAX

Formac Publishing Company Limited recognizes the support of the Province of Nova Scotia through Nova Scotia Business Inc. We are pleased to work in partnership with the Province to develop and promote our creative industries of Nova Scotia. We acknowledge the support of the Canada Council for the Arts, which last year invested $153 million to bring the arts to Canadians throughout the country. This project has been made possible in part by the Government of Canada.

Design by Meghan Collins
Food styling by Amanda Langley
Photography by Jen Partridge, Partridge Photography
with the exception of page 80 Shutterstock.

Library and Archives Canada Cataloguing in Publication

McCallum, Wendy, author
       No more junk food! : 80+ delicious recipes to replace popular processed foods / Wendy McCallum, RHN.

Includes index.
Previous title: Real food for real families.
ISBN 978-1-4595-0457-8 (paperback)

       1. Cooking. 2. Cooking (Natural foods). 3. Cookbooks.
I. Title.

TX714.M2752 2016   641.5   C2016-902061-4

Formac Publishing Company Limited
5502 Atlantic Street
Halifax, Nova Scotia, Canada
B3H 1G4
www.formac.ca

Printed and bound in Korea.

Acknowledgements

Thanks to all my real kid testers, big and small, who took a leap of faith and tried new things, and a special thanks to Miss Mae and Ida, and their mama, the "other Wendy," who tried just about everything I came up with and who liked just about everything they tried.

A sincere thanks to my editor and friend, and fellow believer in the power of real food, Meghan Collins. You put your whole heart into this little book and it shows on every page.

Jen Partridge and Amanda Langley: thanks to you both, my food came to life in your talented hands!

Thanks to every family member and friend I cautiously shared this crazy venture with who offered me enthusiastic words of support and encouragement — you know who you are.

The biggest thank you of all to my very own amazingly awesome real family, Rob, Duncan and Georgia, for all your tasting, testing and positive feedback. Thank you for not complaining once when we had breakfast for dinner and cocktail food for breakfast for weeks on end. Mostly though, thanks for teaching me that the secret ingredient, in life and good food, is always love.

Contents

Introduction

This is not a gourmet cookbook, and I'm not a chef. I'm just a regular mom who figured out — through years of trial and error — how to make great-tasting, healthy, real food and, more importantly, how to get her kids to actually eat it!

It wasn't easy, and it sure didn't happen overnight. Like a lot of moms out there, I did my very best to "do it all" for many years, by which I really mean "do everything I thought everyone else expected me to do." "Doing it all" encompassed two babies, a husband and a busy law practice. And, like many moms, I realized I couldn't actually do it all very well. Something had to give. So I identified the thing that meant the least to me but took the most of me, and left my law career. Then I took a leap of faith (and a pay cut!) and went back to school to study natural food, which I was starting to get pretty passionate about.

During that crazy stage of babies and partnership and clients, I started thinking critically about what I was feeding my family. I knew there was plenty of room for improvement, but I also knew I couldn't realistically handle more than one change at a time, given our busy lives. So that's how I did it — one change at a time. Once I had a handle on a new habit, I would start working on another change.

The first thing I did was consciously include at least one fruit or veggie at each snack or meal, so I could feel confident that we were all getting at least five servings each day. After a couple of months, I switched to buying organic and/or local produce whenever it was available and affordable. A few months later, I slowly replaced the prepackaged convenience foods we had relied on with more-natural, fewer-ingredient prepackaged convenience foods. At some point, I started experimenting with dairy-free recipes, when I noticed that a few of us McCallums seemed to feel better with less dairy in

our diets. About six months after that, I introduced more vegetarian protein into our diet. In the last few years, I've been trying to feed us all whole, natural, unprocessed food.

These recipes are the culmination of more than eight years of my tinkering and experimenting with recipes, as I tried to make them tastier, simpler, healthier and — most importantly — kid-friendly. My recipes are straightforward. I don't use fancy techniques or obscure ingredients (if any are unfamiliar, you can check the Pantry List, page 12). To make things even easier, many of these dishes can be frozen for convenient, quick dinners on busy weeknights. I've identified the nutritional pitfalls of many common processed convenience foods that Canadian families favour, then offered easy and healthy real-food alternatives for you to try.

Eight years of feeding and parenting two children, and discovering through trial and error what it takes to raise healthy eaters in our modern Canadian food system, taught me lots of tips and tricks. Some of my suggestions may be strategies you've learned yourself, while others may be new to you. Making one change at a time is the secret to success. Choose one or two recipes or tips that resonate with you, and start with those.

What's my family-food philosophy? I'm a big believer in balance, and in letting kids enjoy tasty food and have a treat now and then, but I am also dedicated to helping parents ensure that their kids are eating a variety of healthy whole foods.

And what do I mean by "whole" or "real" food? If

you see it on your plate and you can imagine it growing or living in nature, it's probably a whole food (think broccoli, eggs, chicken or brown rice). Most whole foods are one-ingredient foods, but some whole foods can be made with combined whole-food ingredients. If it's a prepared food, look at the label and ask yourself if there are five or fewer ingredients, and if you can pronounce, recognize and imagine them in nature. If so, it probably qualifies as a whole food. Real, whole foods are naturally high in essential nutrients and fibre, and low in sugars, unhealthy fats and sodium.

On the other hand, if it contains ingredients you can't pronounce, added sugars, or refined flours, it's probably not real food, but rather processed food, which tends to be low in nutrients and fibre and what might be characterized as "junk".

Canadian families are not eating enough real, whole food. The childhood-obesity rate in Canada is a shocking 31.5 per cent in 5 to 17 year-olds, (according to a 2012 Statistics Canada publication), and we are raising the first generation of Canadian children who are expected to have shorter lives than their parents. This shortened lifespan is strongly associated with the amount of high-sugar, high-fat and high-sodium processed foods our children are eating.

A 2007 report found that 50 per cent of Canadian children aged 4 to 18 are not getting the minimum recommended daily serving of fruits and veggies, and an earlier 2004 study indicated a whopping 23 per cent of Canadians' calorie intake was coming from "other foods" not falling into one of the four food groups. In other words, almost one quarter of the calories our families are consuming contain no real nutritional value!

Transitioning your family to real, whole food can be daunting, especially if you have heavily relied on processed food or you have extra-picky eaters at home. It's worth the effort to change, though, and you can do it! If you need a parental pep talk to get you started, remember these key points:

When it comes to setting an example, parents have more influence on their children than any other people. You can teach your children a critical lifelong health habit that can literally shape the rest of their lives. They are watching you. They see you drinking pop, skipping meals and picking at your own vegetables! They also see you exercising, eating salads and cooking healthy meals at home!

You, not your kids, are in charge of the food. You buy the groceries, choose the recipes and cook the meals. Most importantly, you set the patterns. If you set healthy patterns from the start, you'll never have to struggle with breaking bad habits. A child who has never eaten white rice at home will never expect it at home, while a child who has been through a fast-food drive-through once will want to do again.

It is your job to persevere. It sometimes takes 10 to 15 tries before kids will eat and admit to liking a new food. You wouldn't give up on changing other undesirable behaviours after a couple of tries, so why give up on selective eating?

Here's an analogy that motivates the parents I speak with: The first time you hear from the daycare staff that your perfect toddler has bitten another child, what do you do? You panic, terrified you are raising a sociopath, and you come up with a fail-safe strategy to ensure that it never happens again. Which of course it does. The very next day. So you up the ante, lay down the law, promise rewards and cross your fingers for as long as it takes. When there's finally a day without biting, you celebrate, praise and reward your child. When you hear the dreaded news of a relapse, after a streak of perfect behaviour, you do not throw your hands up in the air and think to hell with it. Nope, you parent up, buckle down and start all over again. But, when it comes to healthy eating habits, many of us admit defeat the third time our children announce they won't eat anything green. We can't give up! Healthy eating is the most important health habit we are responsible for teaching our children.

MAMA'S LITTLE HELPER: MEAL PLANNING 101

If you don't already plan your meals each week, I'm making it my mission to convince you to try it. Here's why:

It will save you money. In fact, it is the key to healthy eating on a budget.
It will make grocery shopping quick and painless.
It will ensure variety in your family's food.
It will reduce waste.
It can reduce the time you spend cooking.
It will reduce significantly the amount of processed or convenience foods your family eats.
Most importantly, it can preserve your sanity.

How do you do it? It's easy:

- Get a template for a week's worth of planning (go to www.formac.ca/realfood for a downloadable Keeping It Real Meal Planning template).
- Look at your family calendar and note any activities or events that will make it difficult to cook certain meals on certain days or to cook for certain family members to eat with the rest of the family. Record these on your meal planner.
- Go through a book of healthy recipes, such as this one, and choose some simple meals to try on the days you will have time to cook from scratch. Note the recipes on your planner.
- Don't waste what you have. Check your freezer and pantry. Do you have any ingredients or foods that need to be used? Incorporate them into this week's plan!
- Don't reinvent the wheel at every meal. At least half of your dinner options should be recipes that you've made successfully before.
- On days where you know you will be rushed, either pencil in a healthy homemade fast-food option (see Happier at Home, page 62) or choose a recipe you can make in advance and freeze, making a note on the planner that you need to take it out to defrost that morning.
- Fill in breakfasts and lunches, making use of leftovers from previous dinners, and note when you might need to double a recipe to provide an extra meal for the next day or evening.
- Include a list of family snacks for the week, including fruit and veggies, and note any recipes to make in advance on the weekend.
- Go through your meal plan once it's complete, and make a detailed grocery list of everything you need.
- Go shopping and get everything you need on Friday or Saturday.
- Schedule a morning, afternoon or evening on the weekend to make whatever you need/want to prepare in advance.
- Remember to check the meal plan every evening to make sure you know what's coming up the next day.
- Be flexible. Stuff happens. Always have the fixings for a couple of healthy fast-food options in the pantry, just in case.
- Treat yourself to a parents' night out with all the money you saved. You deserve it!

The same parenting strategies that lead to success with other behaviours will work with food. Repeat, reinforce, praise! Your kids want to please you, so make sure you find a reason to praise their efforts to eat healthy whenever you can. Always combine your praise with education — tell them why this or that food is good for them. Not sure why? Google it!

Kids are empowered by choice. Get them involved in family food, by giving them their own veggie patch in the garden or a healthy meal to plan once a week. Let your children choose one of the recipes in this book, then help you cook it. Your job is to teach them how to choose nutritious foods, not to simply tell them what to eat.

Dig in and persevere. If you want to raise happy, healthy kids, teaching good eating habits is part of your job as a parent. Give it the same dedication you would give to any other fundamental aspect of parenting. I can't promise miracles, but I can promise that you will see slow and steady positive changes.

The rest of this chapter provides strategies to get you organized and prepared, and some tips as to the hows and whats of talking to your kids about eating real food. And the recipes will get you all off to a good start.

A WINNING COMBINATION: COMPLEX CARBS, PROTEINS AND HEALTHY FATS

A terrific way for kids (and adults) to eat is to combine healthy macronutrients (complex carbohydrates, proteins and healthy fats) in every snack and meal. Combining these macronutrients supports balanced eating, long-lasting energy and healthy, moderated blood-sugar levels.

Here's how it works:

COMPLEX CARBOHYDRATES are found in vegetables and whole grains. Other healthy but technically simple carbs are found in fruit, which is high in fibre and nutrients. Carbohydrates are our children's best energy source.

HEALTHY PROTEINS are found in foods such as

Drive-Through Dilemmas!

Parents often ask me how they can respond to their children's complaints that "so-and-so gets to go to McDonald's" or "so-and-so always gets a treat in her lunch" or "everyone orders from the cafeteria on Fridays." Just a little reminder: You are still in charge. You set the rules and the boundaries when it comes to family food. Be strong and set clear boundaries from the beginning. You and your children will reap the benefits for life. Shortly after my two children started school, they came home asking for a DunkARoo. I had no idea what these were, which quickly led to a reconnaissance mission at the grocery store. I was absolutely appalled to learn what a DunkARoo was (a graham cracker dipped in icing) and that five-year-olds were actually bringing these to school. I promptly told my two, in no uncertain terms, that DunkARoos were junk and I would never buy them, and my kids never asked again. The thing is, I'm hard-core about junk, especially junk in the middle of a school day when my kids need to fuel themselves to focus for another three or four hours. When your children start school, explain why a healthy lunch is so important for energy, focus and learning. Let them know that they might find a treat in their lunchboxes occasionally, but it won't happen every day. Decide how many times you want them to visit the cafeteria in a week, month or year, and let them know that in advance. If they know they only get to eat cafeteria food once a year at Christmas, they'll stop asking you pretty darn quick. If you never take your children to McDonald's, they'll never ask you to go to the drive-through, trust me. (But they will probably still ask Grandma!)

When it comes to food, sometimes being a hard-core parent is what it takes to keep your family healthy.

preservative-free lean meats, cold-water fish, free-range eggs, beans and legumes, quinoa and other high-protein grains, unsweetened yogourt, nuts and seeds (and their butters) and organic tofu. Proteins are the building blocks of the human body. Children need a healthy supply of protein for proper growth and daily cell repair.

HEALTHY FATS are found in nuts and seeds (and their butters). They are also found in liquid vegetable oils (two of my favourites are flax and olive oil), coconut oil (a healthy saturated fat, which can be used in high-heat cooking), ground flaxseeds, avocados, wild salmon and cold-water fish, and good-quality omega-3 supplements. Healthy fats are crucial to good health, for maintaining cell and nerve health, and for brain development.

It's especially easy to favour bread products and other grain-based carbohydrates when preparing snacks and lunches, because they're portable and easy to grab and go. The problem is that while kids get most of their energy from carbohydrates, children need more than just grains (even the whole kind) to meet their nutritional needs.

Kids need to consume other healthy forms of carbohydrates — such as vegetables and fruit — to ensure they are getting a wide variety of vitamins and minerals.

The best way to always ensure that your children are getting the full spectrum of the macronutrients and micronutrients they need is to combine a little protein and healthy fats with varied, healthy carbs. If you can get into this habit, your kids will also benefit from a slower release of sugar into their bloodstreams, because protein and fat are digested more slowly than carbs on their own. For example, a breakfast made up of balanced macronutrients (egg, whole wheat toast and nut butter) will keep kids going until their next balanced snack at recess. Pop-Tarts or white-flour muffins will lead to hungry kids before the first bell.

Give macronutrient combining a try for a few

HEALTHY EATING ON A BUDGET

Healthy eating on a budget can be tough. Fresh whole foods often cost more than their processed counterparts. But with good planning, we really can eat great-quality food and keep the grocery bills reasonable, too. Here are a few tips for keeping healthy eating affordable, one step at a time:

BEFORE YOU SHOP:

Plan, plan, plan: I cannot oversell the importance of planning. It may take half an hour, but it will save you at least three hours in extra trips to the grocery store and in prep time. Do the week's meal plan before you go shopping (see Mama's Little Helper: Meal Planning 101, page 7).

AT THE STORE:

Look high and low — literally — on the shelves. The most expensive items are almost always placed at eye level, while the bargains sit above and below. Stick to your list. This is crucial. Seven out of every ten purchases are impulse buys. Avoid that trap by knowing exactly what you need.

BACK AT HOME:

Bake with your kids. It lets you control the ingredients and freshness of the foods, it's often much cheaper than buying premade treats and it provides quality time to talk about food with your kids! Cook a large-batch meal every weekend and freeze half, or use leftovers for weekday lunches. Plan and cook with local and seasonal produce, which is often cheaper and fresher than the imports, and your choices help support nearby farmers. Eat vegetarian a couple of meals a week, then use the money you've saved to splurge on best-quality, grass-fed meat from your local market or butcher. Freeze, freeze, freeze. Not only does this let you take advantage of bulk deals and sales on healthy items, it can make your life much easier! A few things you might not know you can easily freeze: brown rice, cooked beans, hummus, pesto and leftover fresh herbs (purée with a little olive oil before freezing). Good luck, fellow penny-pinchers! Try these tips for a couple of weeks and you will be amazed at how much money you can save with a little planning.

days, even though it takes a little effort. Trust me, it's worth it, and it gets easier with practice. It's a pretty effective tool for improving the mood and energy levels of cranky exhausted parents, too!

Many of the recipes in this cookbook help get you started, since they're designed with a healthy balance of complex carbs, proteins and healthy fat.

ORGANIC OR NOT?

Whether or not you buy organic produce and/or how much organic food you buy is a personal choice. This decision is often based on a number of factors such as your household income, environmental concerns, availability of the foods, concerns about genetically modified foods and convenience. Given the alleged health risks of pesticide ingestion for young children, I encourage you to do what you reasonably can to reduce your children's exposure.

"If I can't afford to buy all organic produce, is there any point in buying just some organic?" It's a question I'm often asked and, in my opinion, it's worth doing. Certain fruit and veggies are either so sprayed or so thin-skinned that all the washing in the world won't significantly reduce their pesticide content. Other types are less contaminated, so they're a much safer non-organic choice. It's easy to find the top offenders — Google "dirty dozen organic" and you'll be able to print off a current list (it changes regularly).

Take the list when you shop, and look for organic versions of the dirty dozen, price them and decide if you think they are worth it, given the pesticide concern. Some of the foods on the list will be much easier to find as organic foods than others, and this may change what you regularly stock at home. Your kids may love grapes, for example, which are currently in the dirty dozen. Organic grapes are not only quite expensive, but they are difficult to find, so you may want to only buy organic grapes when the price is right or, at minimum, make non-organic grapes an occasional treat instead of a staple.

TEACHING KIDS TO EAT LOCAL

Our industrial food system is failing us. It's producing genetically modified, chemically treated, lower nutrient food, and we can't sustain it. It sounds drastic, but frankly, this unsustainable system is destroying the planet.

That's why it is so important to talk to your children, whatever their ages, about the food on your table, so you can work together to incorporate more whole, local foods into your family's diet.

Here's why (in simple kid-speak) eating local is better:
It just plain tastes better.
Local food is much fresher, often picked the day

before market, so it's got lots more of the good-for-you stuff (nutrients) in it.

Eating local helps you save the planet. Food from your local farmers only has to travel from those farms to your table, not from another country or even another continent. Each long trip requires a lot of fuel and creates a lot of pollution!

Buying local helps keep your nearby farms alive. The more foods we buy that are produced close to home, the easier it is for our farmers to keep farming.

Many fun family activities present wonderful teaching opportunities about local foods. Here are some ideas to get you started:

Take a family trip to a local farmers' market. Explore it together, choose local foods, then plan and cook a meal together from all-local foods.

Consider joining a Community Shared Agriculture Agreement (CSA) with a local farm. This is a terrific way for your family to support local farming by making a commitment to purchase in advance. A wonderful variety of local foods will magically find its way into your kitchen, and you and your children will have loads of fun identifying and trying new foods and tastes!

Get your garden on! Start planning a family garden. Square-foot gardening is one of the easiest and most fail-safe ways to garden, and it's really kid-friendly. You can even garden on a balcony or deck. When you plant a veggie garden at home, you've gone about as local as you can go!

As a treat, you can research and visit one of the restaurants in your area that features local foods. You may be surprised at what delicious gourmet foods are out there, grown by your neighbours!

Presentation Is Key!
KIDS EAT WITH THEIR EYES FIRST

Guess what? It's not just common sense. Colourful, fun and enticing meals attract kids. It's proven science. A study published in 2012 by researchers at Cornell University concluded that children prefer more colour, variety and creativity in food presentation than adults do. So get creative and increase the odds that your kids will try new foods.

Colourful natural foods provide diverse nutrients, so eat that rainbow! Dress up your child's plate with fun shapes, colours and designs. There are handy kitchen tools that make this easier: spiral and ribbon veggie peelers, skewers, cookie cutters, fun ice cube trays, bento boxes and brightly coloured dinnerware can all contribute to interesting presentation.

Pantry List

A few of the ingredients in my recipes might be new to you, but they are all easy to find and use. Here's a list of what they are and where to find them.

ingredient	what it is	where to find it
apple butter	Wonderful, naturally sweet alternative to jam, made with natural apples and no added sugar.	natural food section of conventional grocery store natural food store
apple cider vinegar	A vinegar with lots of positive health properties. Always look for a brand that is "with mother" to ensure the nutritious bits haven't been filtered out. The bottle will clearly state this on the label.	vinegar aisle or natural food section of conventional grocery store natural food store
aluminum-free baking powder	Ingested aluminum has been linked to health issues such as Alzheimer's and ADD, so why take the chance? Use aluminum-free baking powder.	natural food store natural food section of some grocery stores (Bob's Red Mill brand, for example), or through specialty companies such as Epicure in Canada
arrowroot powder	A natural thickener made from the arrowroot plant, this comes in a flour form and can replace cornstarch in recipes, which is generally made from genetically modified (GM) corn.	natural food store
brown rice pasta	A gluten-free pasta made from brown rice. Cook it, rinse it well, then reheat it under hot water for best results.	natural food section of conventional grocery store natural food store
coconut milk	Available in a can or often in a carton, this makes a great dairy alternative in creamy soups or casseroles. Look for a reduced-fat version for a lower calorie milk.	ethnic and/or natural food section of conventional grocery store
coconut oil	A great oil for high-heat cooking, coconut oil is naturally antibacterial, antifungal and anti-inflammatory, and stable at a high temperature. Virgin coconut oil will impart a slight coconut flavour; nonvirgin will not. Use it for cooking and melt it as a replacement for vegetable oil in baking.	natural food store natural food section of conventional grocery store

ingredient	what it is	where to find it
edamame	Edamame is the Japanese name for young soybeans. Buy these green beans frozen (shelled or unshelled) and defrost and heat for a quick source of protein.	freezer section of natural food section of conventional grocery store
flax oil	Derived from flax, this oil is a great source of omega-3. A delicate fat, it should be kept in the fridge and never heated. Great in salad dressings.	cooler of natural food section of conventional grocery store
ground flaxseed or flax meal	Flaxseed is a great source of healthy omega-3 fat and fibre, but its nutrients are best absorbed when ground. Buy flaxseed and grind it yourself, or buy pre-ground flaxseed (meal). Store it in the fridge.	natural food store natural food section of conventional grocery store
Herbamare	A brand of seasoning salt that adds a subtle flavour to dishes.	natural food section of conventional grocery store natural food store
kale	My favourite dark leafy green vegetable, kale is a nutritional powerhouse. Just remove the thick stem and chop; add to recipes as you would spinach.	leafy greens section of conventional grocery store local farmers' market
low-sodium soy sauce or tamari	Chinese soy sauce usually contains wheat as well as soy, while Japanese tamari is usually wheat- (and gluten-) free. Both can be high in sodium, so look for a low-sodium option. My favourite is Bragg's Soy Seasoning, which is lower sodium, wheat- and gluten-free and made from non–genetically modified soybeans.	natural food store natural food section of conventional grocery store
nutritional (or vegetarian) yeast flakes	Normally fortified with vitamin B12, this is a deactivated yellow flaked yeast that imparts a cheesy, tangy flavour to dishes. Great for those avoiding or reducing dairy! Yummy as a popcorn topping too.	natural food section of conventional grocery store natural food store
plain greek yogourt	A thick yogourt that is often very high in protein. Look for a brand that has 18 to 20 grams protein per serving, and no added sugar.	dairy cooler section of conventional grocery store
soba noodles	Typically made of buckwheat and gluten-free, these are hearty, tasty noodles that turn soup into a meal. If you are avoiding gluten, check the label to ensure other gluten-containing grains are not ingredients.	natural food section of conventional grocery store natural food store Asian grocery store

ingredient	what it is	where to find it
spelt flour	A grain in the wheat family, spelt is lower in gluten and easier to digest for many gluten-sensitive people. It's easy to use in the place of wheat in most recipes.	natural food section of conventional grocery store natural food store
stevia	A natural sweetener derived from the stevia plant, this is available in liquid or powder form. It has only a negligible effect on blood sugar.	natural food section of conventional grocery store natural food store
"sunbutter" or sunflower seed butter	Similar to peanut butter but made with ground sunflower seeds, this can be used as a "school-safe" substitute whenever a recipe calls for peanut or other nut butter.	natural food section of conventional grocery store natural food store
tahini or tahina	Ground sesame seed paste that is a source of healthy fat and is used in Middle Eastern cooking. Keep it cool and use it in stir-fry sauces and salad dressings.	ethnic and/or natural food section of conventional grocery store natural food store
toasted sesame oil	I love the flavour that just a small amount of this oil will impart to a recipe. Wonderful addition to simple stir-fried veggies.	natural food or Asian grocery store
tofu (silken, soft or firm)	Made from soybeans, tofu is a cheap, complete protein. As most nonorganic soybeans have been genetically modified, look for organic or non-GM soy tofu. Once opened, cover tofu with water and store in an airtight container in the fridge. Tofu will keep for three to five days if the water is changed daily. Silken tofu has a very different consistency from firm tofu, so be sure to use the specific type called for in the recipe.	cooler section of natural food section of conventional grocery store cooler section of natural food store silken tofu may be packaged so as not to require refrigeration and found on conventional grocery store shelves
unsweetened almond, soy or rice milk	These are all dairy alternatives that can be substituted for cow's milk in most recipes. Almond milk is my favourite due to its sweet taste and milk-like consistency. Beware of vanilla, chocolate or other flavoured varieties as they are normally much higher in sugar.	natural food section of conventional grocery store
whole wheat pastry flour	This finer flour is great for recipes that make fluffier, lighter baked goods such as waffles and scones.	natural food store

HEALTHY BREAKFASTS

Kids (and adults, too) need to eat healthy breakfasts for a whole host of reasons. First of all, when we wake up, we have been fasting all night, so our blood sugar is low. We really do need breakfast to break the night's fast and rev up our digestion, replenish our blood sugar and get our bodies energized for the day ahead.

Studies also show a correlation between eating a healthy breakfast and better academic performance, as well as a relationship between poor nutrition and decreased activity, social interaction, curiosity and focus. Kids who are fuelled better perform better — academically, physically and socially.

On top of all that, breakfast may be the only meal that most of us can control in our children's busy days. Many kids are eating snacks and lunches at daycare or at school, and many families grab dinner on the run between after-school activities. Breakfast is the one meal that almost all of our children eat at home.

Even if we send our kids off with balanced snacks and lunches, it's often hit or miss whether that healthy stuff ever lands in their bellies. You can stand guard at breakfast and ensure that everyone leaves the house properly fuelled for the day.

The problem? Breakfast is rushed and chaotic in most households, and prepackaged convenience foods often seem like a necessary evil. More often than not, these foods are chock full of refined grains, added sugar, salt and loads of not-so-real ingredients.

The solution? Get up a few minutes earlier and (one recipe at a time) establish a go-to family repertoire of healthy, quick and easy breakfasts. It's really that simple. Once you establish a routine, everyone will leave the house nourished and ready for the day. Remember, it takes at least 21 days to form a habit, so get your family eating a healthy, homemade breakfast for at least three weeks straight, in order to start creating a lifelong habit. Keep a sticker chart or calendar that celebrates your family's success, if that helps — whatever keeps you on track!

This next chapter offers an array of healthy, easy choices. Some you can prepare in five minutes, others you can prepare in advance, then pull straight from the fridge to the breakfast table or even the car. Find four or five recipes that suit your family and get started!

No More
DRIVE-THROUGH
BREAKFAST

The breakfast sandwich has become a quintessential North American breakfast fast food. Luckily for all of us, it's one of the simplest things to make in a healthier version at home. It's so simple, in fact, that it's a bit of a stretch to even call this a recipe!

AVOCADO AND EGGER *instead!*

GATHER

100% whole wheat English muffin

1 large egg

1 tablespoon shredded skim mozzarella or white cheddar cheese

$\frac{1}{8}$ avocado

1 slice nitrite-free ham, chicken or turkey (optional, omit for a vegetarian breakfast)

*Optional healthy boosts include extra veggies such as baby spinach and sliced tomato.

MAKE

Toast English muffin. Meanwhile, in skillet over medium heat, combine egg and cheese and cook, scrambling slightly. Smear avocado on toasted muffin half, then top with ham and egg mixture (and any extra veggies you can squeeze in) and other muffin half.

Serves 1.

Get Your Egg on!

Eggs are an almost-perfect food — each egg contains only 70 or so calories, about 6 grams of protein and 14 essential nutrients. Eggs also contain choline, which is very important for brain development, and antioxidants, which are believed to protect our eyes from sun damage. To top it all off, they are one of the most "bioavailable" foods humans can eat — meaning it's really easy for our digestive systems to tap into their goodness. Get crackin'!

No More
FAST FOOD BURRITOS!

VEGETARIAN OPTION

DAIRY-FREE OPTION

GLUTEN-FREE OPTION

NUT-FREE OPTION

These burritos are quick and easy — and far from the average high-calorie take-out versions, these babies are packed with fibre, iron, protein, healthy fat and antioxidants. Nothing beats them for nutrition and convenience!

BREAKFAST BLACK BEAN BURRITO instead!

GATHER

1 clove garlic, crushed

1 teaspoon chopped onion

½ cup fresh, finely chopped spinach

¼ cup black beans, rinsed and drained

1 large egg

¼ cup pure liquid egg whites

1 tablespoon shredded cheese*

¼ avocado

2 teaspoons mild salsa (optional)

2 small whole wheat tortillas with less than 100 calories each**

*For a dairy-free option, eliminate cheese.

**For a gluten-free option, choose brown-rice or corn tortillas.

MAKE

In nonstick or lightly sprayed skillet over medium heat, sauté garlic and onion until softened. Stir in spinach and beans and cook until spinach has wilted. With fork, gently scramble in egg, egg whites and cheese and cook, stirring occasionally, until cooked through. Meanwhile, spread avocado and salsa, if desired, over each tortilla. Scrape half of the egg mixture along one edge of each tortilla, then wrap up, burrito-style.

Serves 2.

"Eating this gives me powers. I could ride a buckaroo all day."
— William, age 7

No More
FAST FOOD BREAKFAST!

This easy egg recipe works as well for dinner as it does for breakfast. A one-dish, budget-friendly, last-minute meal, it's great for a busy weeknight or a lazy Sunday brunch, served with carrots on the side.

EASY EGG PIE instead!

GATHER

1 tablespoon extra-virgin olive oil

4 unpeeled potatoes, scrubbed, precooked and sliced

1 clove garlic, crushed

½ large onion, diced

Chopped veggies such as broccoli, bell peppers, mushrooms and tomatoes (optional)

4 large eggs

1¾ cups cow's, soy, rice or unsweetened almond milk

½ teaspoon dried marjoram

½ teaspoon basil

¼ teaspoon paprika

⅓ cup nutritional yeast

¼ teaspoon each salt and pepper

1 cup chopped fresh or frozen spinach (if frozen, thawed and drained)

Shredded cheese (optional, omit for dairy-free option)

MAKE

In cast-iron skillet, heat oil over medium heat. Sauté potatoes, garlic, onion and chopped veggies, if desired, until softened and browned.

In bowl, whisk together eggs, milk, marjoram, basil, paprika, nutritional yeast, salt and pepper. Stir in spinach.

Spread potato mixture evenly over pan, pressing down to form a "crust." Pour egg mixture over top. Sprinkle with cheese (if using). Bake in 350°F oven until centre is set, about 35 minutes.

Serves 6.

Cooking with Cast Iron!

I love cooking with a good cast-iron pan. The food absorbs iron from the pan, increasing the iron content of the dish, and the more the pan gets used, the better the food from the pan tastes. If you don't have a cast-iron pan, you can use any ovenproof skillet for the Easy Egg Pie.

No More
FROZEN HASH BROWNS!

Make these at home on a weekend morning, and you'll be amazed at how many veggies you can inconspicuously squeeze into one little potato patty. Start with the basic recipe, then experiment by replacing some of the potato with shredded zucchini, carrot or parsnip. It's easy! Great for breakfast, these hash browns also serve up a savoury side at dinnertime. If you're feeling bold, add fresh herbs such as rosemary, chives or oregano. A good food processor fitted with a grater attachment makes these a breeze, and using two skillets speeds up the cooking time. Enjoy!

HOMEMADE HASH BROWNS instead!

GATHER

2 cups grated peeled sweet
   potatoes

2 cups grated peeled potatoes

2 large eggs, beaten

1 clove garlic, crushed

½ cup finely chopped onion

¼ teaspoon sea salt

⅛ teaspoon pepper

½ cup ground flaxseed

1 to 2 teaspoons coconut oil

MAKE

In large bowl, combine sweet and white potatoes (if mixture is wet, transfer to colander over sink and squeeze out excess liquid, then return mixture to bowl). Stir in eggs, garlic, onion, salt and pepper to coat. Stir in flaxseed and let stand until flaxseed has absorbed some of the liquid, 3 to 5 minutes.

Meanwhile, in cast-iron or heavy skillet, heat 1 teaspoon of the coconut oil over medium heat and swirl to coat bottom of pan. Reduce heat to medium-low.

Using small lightly greased scoop or ladle, spoon in mounds of mixture, about ¼ cup at a time, then slightly flatten each (4 or 5 patties per pan). Cover and cook, turning once after 10 minutes and checking to prevent burning, for 20 minutes. Repeat with remaining mixture, adding more oil to pan, if necessary. Serve hot.

Serves 8.

VEGETARIAN &
VEGAN OPTION

DAIRY-FREE
OPTION

NUT-FREE
OPTION

FREEZER-FRIENDLY

No More
FROZEN WAFFLES!

Leave the frozen store-bought waffles behind and make your own! I make a big batch of waffles most Saturday mornings, then freeze the leftovers to pop into the toaster on busy weekday mornings. This recipe is healthy, delicious and high in fibre. To push the nutritional value up even higher, add berries or grated apple or pear. To add protein to the meal, serve with a dollop of greek yogourt or a side of scrambled eggs.

CINNAMON FLAX TOASTER WAFFLES instead!

GATHER

2 large eggs, beaten

1¾ cups cow's, almond or soy milk

¼ cup unsweetened applesauce

¼ cup olive oil

2 tsp maple syrup

1 teaspoon vanilla extract

1 teaspoon cinnamon

1 cup whole wheat pastry flour

½ cup flaxseed meal

¼ cup wheat germ

¼ cup all-purpose flour

4 teaspoons aluminum-free baking
    powder

¼ teaspoon salt

No More Jemima syrups (optional,
    pages 26–27)

Plain Greek yogourt (optional)

Suntella (optional, page 44)

MAKE

In large bowl, whisk together eggs, milk, applesauce, oil, maple syrup, vanilla and cinnamon.

Beat or whisk in whole wheat pastry flour, flaxseed meal, wheat germ, all-purpose flour, baking powder and salt until smooth.

In batches of about ½ cup, pour batter into waffle iron and cook until crisp and golden brown. Serve with a No More Jemima syrup, yogourt or Suntella, if desired.

To freeze: Separate leftover waffles into quarters, layer between waxed paper to prevent sticking, then transfer to freezer bags. Freeze for up to a month or so. Pop frozen waffles into toaster and toast until browned and warmed through.

Makes about 8 large waffles.

"These are awesomely delicious."
– Paige, age 8

Flax Facts: It's Flax-Tastic!

You may notice that I've included ground flaxseed (or flaxseed flour or meal) and flax oil in many of the recipes in this cookbook. For our digestive systems to best absorb flaxseed nutrients, the flaxseed needs to be ground into meal or pressed into oil.

Flaxseed really is a "flax-tastic" natural food. It's a source of omega-3 fatty acids, which are linked with decreased inflammation and heart disease (most of us don't get enough omega-3 fatty acids through our diet). Flaxseed is also a good source of protein, fibre, iron, thiamine and magnesium. Because flaxseed and flax oil contain unstable fatty acids, which can be destroyed when heated to high temperatures and exposed to sunlight, you should store your ground meal and oil in the fridge, and never use them when cooking at a very high temperature. You can also simply start sprinkling these ground flax-tastic seeds on everything — yogourt, oatmeal, smoothies and salads!

"I love these pancakes. Yaaay!"

– Tyler, age 2½

No More
PANCAKE MIX!

VEGETARIAN OPTION

DAIRY-FREE OPTION

NUT-FREE OPTION

FREEZER-FRIENDLY OPTION

Better Pancakes are a simple, delicious and economical breakfast treat, and so much healthier than the alternative from a box. If you have leftovers from Saturday morning, you can freeze them to reheat during the week, or you can plan ahead by making a double batch. Experiment by adding grated apple, chopped banana, blueberries or strawberries to pump up the nutritional value.

BETTER PANCAKES instead!

GATHER

1½ cups whole wheat flour

½ cup all-purpose flour

⅓ cup ground flaxseed

¼ cup oat bran

¼ cup granulated sugar

4 teaspoons aluminum-free baking powder

1 teaspoon salt

1 teaspoon cinnamon

2 large eggs, beaten

1½ cups almond, soy or cow's milk

¼ cup extra-virgin olive oil

½ cup (about) water

Sliced fruit (optional)

Plain Greek yogourt (optional)

No More Jemima Syrup
(optional, pages 26–27)

MAKE

In bowl, whisk together whole wheat flour, all purpose flour, flaxseed, bran, sugar, baking powder, salt and cinnamon. Stir in eggs, milk and oil until blended. Stir in water until desired pourable consistency. Into large nonstick or lightly oiled pan over medium heat, pour about ⅓ to ½ a cup at a time, depending on how big you like your pancakes, and cook one at a time and cook until surface is bubbling. Carefully flip and cook until golden brown. Serve with fruit, yogourt and/or No More Jemima Syrup, if desired.

Serves 6.

No More
JEMIMA!

Instead of an artificial breakfast syrup, I prefer to use a little of the real thing (even though maple syrup, while natural, is still sugar). Sometimes I choose an even healthier topping alternative. These fruit-based syrups are much higher in fibre and nutrients than artificial syrups, and lower in refined sugar.

Great over waffles and pancakes, these syrups are delicious anytime — yummy on oatmeal with some pumpkin seeds or walnuts sprinkled over top, and equally delicious poured over yogourt!

Berries are their main ingredient, so these are great lower-sugar alternatives to artificial and real maple syrup. You can substitute one berry for another or make your own mix of berries — either fresh or frozen — to vary the flavours. My kids love this stuff!

BETTER BERRY SYRUP *instead!*

GATHER

1 cup fresh or frozen berries (any
  type, or combination of types)

1 cup water

2 tablespoons maple syrup

2 tablespoons arrowroot powder
  or cornstarch

1 teaspoon vanilla extract

1/8 teaspoon cinnamon

MAKE

In blender, combine all ingredients and blend until smooth. Pour into saucepan and bring to a boil, stirring. Remove from heat and whisk until thickened, about 3 minutes.

Refrigerate leftovers in airtight container (syrup will thicken when chilled). Rewarm on stove before serving. You can also freeze family-size portions to thaw and use on weekday mornings.

Serves 6.

"Better than maple syrup!"
– Mae, age 8

STRAWBERRY BANANA SYRUP *instead!*

GATHER

1 banana

1 cup fresh or frozen strawberries

1 cup water

2 tablespoons maple syrup

2 tablespoons arrowroot powder
  or cornstarch

MAKE

In blender, combine all ingredients and blend until smooth. Pour into saucepan and bring to a boil, stirring. Remove from heat and whisk until thickened, about 3 minutes.

Refrigerate leftovers in airtight container (syrup will thicken when chilled). Rewarm on stove before serving. You can also freeze family-size portions to thaw and use on weekday mornings.

Serves 6.

STRAWBERRY ORANGE SYRUP *instead!*

GATHER

2 teaspoons orange zest

Juice of 1 orange or $1/3$ cup
  orange juice

1 cup fresh or frozen strawberries

$2/3$ cup water

2 tablespoons maple syrup

2 tablespoons arrowroot powder
  or cornstarch

$1/8$ teaspoon cinnamon

MAKE

In blender, combine all ingredients and blend until smooth. Pour into saucepan and bring to a boil, stirring. Remove from heat and whisk until thickened, about 3 minutes.

Refrigerate leftovers in airtight container (syrup will thicken when chilled). Rewarm on stove before serving. You can also freeze family-size portions to thaw and use on weekday mornings.

Serves 6.

VEGAN OPTION

DAIRY-FREE OPTION

GLUTEN-FREE OPTION

NUT-FREE OPTION

FREEZER-FRIENDLY

No More
INSTANT OATMEAL!

Given the opportunity to eat healthy, natural food, the kids will gobble it up. See for yourself! Try serving your hungry child a bowl of oatmeal sweetened with applesauce and sprinkled with walnuts, or a baked oatmeal square with flaxseed and fruit for extra fibre and nutrients. This basic recipe is cheap and delicious, and provides a natural source of healthy omega-3 fatty acids, fibre and protein to really kick-start their day.

QUICK MAPLE FLAX OATMEAL instead!

GATHER

¹/₃ cup quick-cooking rolled oats*

1 tablespoon ground flaxseed

¼ teaspoon cinnamon

²/₃ cup boiling water

2 tablespoons unsweetened
    applesauce

1 teaspoon maple syrup

1 teaspoon chopped nuts or seeds
    (optional)

Berries and/or chopped or grated
    fruit (optional)

*To ensure recipe is gluten-free,
    use certified gluten-free oats, as
    cross-contamination can occur
    in processing.

MAKE

In serving bowl, combine oats, flaxseed and cinnamon. Stir in boiling water and let stand until liquid has been absorbed, 2 to 3 minutes. Stir in applesauce and maple syrup. Top with nuts and berries, if desired.

Serves 1.

"My favourite breakfast other than eggs!"
– Duncan, age 9

On busy mornings, this breakfast will save your bacon (literally, it's vegan)! Make it the night before, pop it into the fridge overnight and reheat in the morning. A yummy treat that's high in healthy protein and fibre, this is comfort food for crazy mornings. My kids love it hot for breakfast and cold as a great grab-and-go snack.

BERRY BAKED OATMEAL instead!

GATHER

2 cups large-flake rolled oats*

½ cup ground flaxseed

¼ cup maple syrup

2 teaspoons cinnamon

2 teaspoons aluminum-free baking
  powder

½ teaspoon sea salt

1 cup frozen berries, chopped if large

1 grated unpeeled apple

¾ cup unsweetened almond milk
  or cow's milk

1 block (340 g) soft silken tofu**

Almond milk, maple syrup or No
  More Jemima Syrup (optional,
  pages 26–27)

Fruit and nuts (optional)

*To ensure recipe is gluten-free,
  use certified gluten-free oats, as
  cross-contamination can occur in
  processing.

**Substitute 1 cup plain Greek
  yogourt to make this soy-free.

MAKE

In large bowl, whisk together oats, flaxseed, cinnamon, baking powder and salt. Stir in berries. In blender or food processor, combine apple, almond or cow's milk, maple syrup and tofu and purée until smooth. Stir into oat mixture until blended. Scrape into greased 8-inch square pan and bake in 350°F oven until top appears dry, 45 to 50 minutes. Cut into 9 squares and serve hot with milk, syrup, fruit or nuts, if desired, or let cool for a cold snack. You can also wrap individual portions and freeze in a freezer-safe container for later use.

Serves 9.

VEGETARIAN &
VEGAN OPTION

DAIRY-FREE
OPTION

GLUTEN-FREE
OPTION

FREEZER-FRIENDLY

No More
HARVEST CRUNCH!

At the risk of being stereotyped as a "natural-food lover," I'm offering this recipe for granola, but, honestly, it's so easy and yummy, I can't resist. Make this with your kids, and let them add or substitute their favourite nuts, seeds and dried fruits. If you mix up a couple of batches before the holidays and throw in some dried cranberries, you can package this granola in decorative jars for the perfect hostess gift. If you print cute holiday jar labels, it makes a great gift for your children's teachers, bus drivers and coaches, too. Delicious alone, with milk, on yogourt or as a homemade muffin topping, this granola doesn't last long in our house. To make it safe to take to school, replace the nuts with more seeds.

BASIC BIRKENSTOCK GRANOLA instead!

GATHER

4 cups large-flake rolled oats*

1 cup chopped nuts (any type
   or combination)

1 cup seeds (try pumpkin,
   sunflower and/or sesame)

½ cup unsweetened shredded
   coconut

1 teaspoon pumpkin pie spice

¾ cup unpasteurized liquid honey or
   maple syrup (or try half of each)**

4 tablespoons melted coconut oil

1 tablespoon toasted sesame oil

1 teaspoon vanilla extract

Chopped dried fruit or raisins
   (optional)

MAKE

In large bowl, stir together oats, nuts, seeds, coconut and spice. In another bowl, whisk together honey, coconut oil, sesame oil and vanilla. Stir into oat mixture. Spread evenly over 2 ungreased non-stick baking sheets (lining with parchment paper makes for easier cleanup) and bake in 325°F oven, stirring every 10 minutes, for 30 minutes. Let cool in pans on racks (granola becomes crunchy as it cools). Stir in dried fruit, if desired, and store in airtight container at room temperature for up to 2 weeks.

Serves 36.

*To ensure recipe is gluten-free, use certified gluten-free oats,
   as cross-contamination can occur in processing.

**Health Canada advises that parents not to feed children under
   the age of one honey, because of a link to infant botulism.

No More
FROOT LOOPS!

You can easily throw out the packaged cereal and take convenience to a whole new level — mix this in a bowl the night before, refrigerate overnight and — presto! — a balanced breakfast or morning snack ready to go. Oats are a great source of protein and fibre, the berries add antioxidants and the almond milk is a hit of calcium. You'll be amazed by the great taste of this simple combination!

OVERNIGHT MUESLI *instead!*

GATHER

2 cups fresh or frozen berries

2 cups almond milk*

1 cup large-flake rolled oats**

2 teaspoons maple syrup

1 teaspoon cinnamon

1 teaspoon vanilla extract

Grated orange zest and/or
   chopped walnuts (optional)

*Use cow's milk or soy milk to
   keep nut-free.

**To ensure recipe is gluten-free,
   use certified gluten-free oats, as
   cross-contamination can occur
   in processing.

MAKE

In large bowl, stir together berries, milk, oats, syrup, cinnamon and vanilla. Cover and refrigerate overnight. Before serving, stir in orange zest and/or walnuts, if desired.

Tip: If you are using frozen berries, thaw them, then add just before serving — not the night before — so the muesli doesn't get mushy. Lord knows, there's nothing worse than soupy muesli!

Serves 4.

No More DRIVE-THROUGH MUFFINS!

The ingredient list is a bit longer than that of most of my recipes, but that's just because I've packed so much real goodness into these Good Morning Muffins. They don't take long to whip up, and are well worth the chopping and grating. Make them in the evening or on the weekend, and freeze them for later. You'll never order a drive-through muffin again!

GOOD MORNING MUFFINS instead!

GATHER

1 apple, finely chopped (unpeeled, if it's organic)

2 cups shredded carrots (about 3 large)

1 cup shredded zucchini (about 1 small)

1¾ cup whole wheat flour

1 cup granulated sugar

¾ cup raisins

¾ cup unsweetened shredded coconut

¼ cup pumpkin seeds

¼ cup sunflower seeds

1 tablespoon cinnamon

2 teaspoons baking soda

2 teaspoons orange zest

½ teaspoon salt

¼ teaspoon ginger

3 large eggs

½ cup melted coconut oil

½ cup unsweetened applesauce

1 teaspoon vanilla extract

MAKE

In large bowl, stir together apple, carrots, zucchini, flour, sugar, raisins, coconut, pumpkin seeds, sunflower seeds, cinnamon, baking soda, orange zest, salt and ginger. In small bowl, lightly beat eggs. Whisk in melted oil, applesauce and vanilla. Stir into apple mixture until combined (do not overmix). With ¼-cup scoop, fill 18 lightly greased muffin tins and bake in 375°F oven until toothpick inserted in centre comes out clean, about 25 minutes.

Makes 18 muffins.

No More
INSTANT MUFFINS!

Muffins are easy to throw together and almost impossible to mess up. This easy, kid-tested recipe makes breakfasts fast and fun. Bake several batches and throw them into the freezer to serve later — with fruit and yogourt at breakfast or in a lunchbox for a healthy recess snack.

BANANA BREAKFAST MUFFINS *instead!*

GATHER

3 ripe or frozen bananas

1 large egg, lightly beaten

¼ cup maple syrup

¼ cup granulated sugar

¼ cup melted coconut oil

1 cup spelt or whole wheat flour

½ cup all-purpose flour

⅓ cup oat bran

1 teaspoon baking soda

1 teaspoon aluminum-free baking
   powder

½ teaspoon salt

9 walnut halves (optional)

MAKE

In small bowl, with fork, mash bananas. Whisk in egg, maple syrup, sugar and melted oil until blended. In large bowl, whisk together whole wheat flour, all-purpose flour, oat bran, baking soda, baking powder and salt. Fold in banana mixture until just combined. Evenly divide into 9 greased muffin tins or paper muffin cups. Garnish each with walnut half if you like. Bake in 375°F oven for 20 minutes.

Makes 9 muffins.

No More
INSTANT BREAKFAST!

Meal replacement drinks are often high in sugar and low in fibre, so in our house, we make smoothies. We call our morning smoothie our "daily flu shot"! Regularly incorporating a nutrient-dense smoothie into your family's day boosts everyone's energy levels and immunity. Even better, most homemade smoothies can be made in less than two minutes! You can add almost anything healthy to the mix, while a touch of natural sweetener can entice even the littlest people to try it! Here's a basic four-person recipe to get you started.

BASIC FAMILY SMOOTHIE *instead!*

GATHER

2 to 3 florets frozen broccoli

1 banana

Handful baby spinach

Handful ice cubes

1 cup cow's, almond, soy or rice milk

1 cup water

1 cup fresh or frozen blueberries or
other berries

1 tablespoon ground flaxseed

1 tablespoon wheat germ
(optional)

Pinch cinnamon or dash vanilla
extract (optional)

Liquid honey, maple syrup or
stevia (optional)

MAKE

In blender, combine all ingredients, as desired, and blend until smooth.

Serves 4.

REAL LUNCHES

Designing healthy and balanced real lunches can be tricky for a whole host of reasons:

- We're often out of our homes for lunch — at work or school — so our midday meals need to be portable.
- We often have nowhere to reheat or refrigerate our lunches, which limits our options.
- As parents, we're often restricted as to what we can send with our school-age kids by no-nut and other allergy-based food policies at many schools.
- Often, our kids have a very limited amount of time to eat at school, so their lunches need to be easy to eat, attractive and yummy or they won't be eaten.
- It's so easy to get stuck in the sandwich rut, which can lead to untouched lunches, day after day, and überfrustration for parents.
- Commercial processed and portable lunch and recess options are everywhere, and the marketing to kids is relentless, leading our kids to beg for what "everyone else is eating."

The key to getting real with your family lunches is preparation and a little creativity. Take it from me — a regular mom with a busy job and not one superhuman power — it can be done. As with everything else, the best approach is step by step, one healthy change at a time.

No More
PREMADE PB&J!

Don't fear the no-nuts rule! This is where sunflower seed butter comes in. Made of crushed sunflower seeds, this butter is both tasty and school-friendly, and a perfect, soy-free, nut-free sandwich spread. Apple butter, a sweet treat made from apples with no added refined sugar, is sunflower seed butter's best friend. Together, they make the SB&A. It's taking over classrooms across the country!

SB&A (SUNBUTTER AND APPLE BUTTER) instead!

GATHER

1 tablespoon sunflower seed butter

1 tablespoon apple butter

2 slices whole wheat bread

Thinly sliced banana or
   strawberries (optional)

MAKE

Spread sunflower seed butter, then apple butter on 1 slice of bread. Top with banana or strawberries, if desired. Sandwich with remaining slice.

Serves 1.

School-Safe Ingredients

The school-safe duo of sunflower seed butter and apple butter is available in the natural food section of most grocery stores and at health food stores. I prefer sunflower seed butter to a soy-nut butter replacement for a couple of reasons: First, if it's not organic soy butter, it's probably made from GM (genetically modified) soybeans, which weird me out a bit. You? Second, soy is full of something called phytoestrogen, which mimics human estrogen in kids' little bodies. This can be good, or possibly bad, depending on the children in question (and, in particular, their gender), so as a general rule, I suggest parents try to limit soy and stick to organic soy whenever possible. Whatever spread you choose, make sure it doesn't contain any extra unwanted ingredients.

No More
FAST FOOD WRAPS!

A quick wrap can be a parent's best friend, and so much better for your family than drive-through wraps that are often minefields of sodium and fat. Portable and compact, homemade wraps can be stuffed with just about anything. The trick is a great sauce. Here are a couple of options that use easy dips and sauces you can make in advance and store in your fridge. In the morning, just spread and assemble for a fresh, healthy wrap!

GRILLED CHICKEN AND TOMATO WRAP *instead!*

GATHER

Less Is More Caesar (page 96)

4 small whole wheat wraps

2 cups spinach or other leafy green

2 small precooked boneless, skinless chicken breasts (or 1 large), sliced

20 cherry or grape tomatoes, halved

MAKE

Spread one-quarter of the dressing on each wrap, top with spinach. Centre several slices of chicken and one-quarter of the tomatoes on each. Tightly roll up (wrap with plastic and keep chilled for lunches).

Serves 4.

HUMMUS PITA WRAP *instead!*

GATHER

1 cup Yummus Hummus (page 92)

4 small whole wheat pitas

2 cups spinach

20 cherry or grape tomatoes, halved

MAKE

Spread one-quarter of the hummus over each pita. Top with spinach and one-quarter of the tomatoes. Tightly roll up (wrap with plastic and keep chilled for lunches).

Serves 4.

VEGETARIAN
OPTION

NUT-FREE
OPTION

SUNBUTTER AND BANANA WRAP *instead!*

GATHER

4 small whole-grain pitas or wraps

4 tablespoons sunflower seed butter

4 small bananas

MAKE

Spread each pita with one-quarter of the sunflower seed butter. Centre 1 peeled banana on each. Tightly roll up (wrap with plastic and keep chilled for lunches).

Serves 4.

GREEK SALAD WRAP WITH TASTY TZATZIKI *instead!*

GATHER

4 small whole wheat pitas

1 cup Tasty Tzatziki (page 97)

1 cup chopped cucumber

1 cup chopped tomato

1 cup chopped green or red bell pepper

½ cup crumbled light feta cheese

⅓ cup sliced black olives (optional)

¼ cup chopped red onion (optional)

MAKE

Spread each pita with one-quarter of the Tasty Tzatziki and top each with one-quarter of the remaining ingredients, as desired. Tightly roll up (wrap with plastic and keep chilled for lunches).

Serves 4.

No More
KRAFT DINNER!

Throw out the box because here is a macaroni alternative made with real, healthy ingredients. You'll feel great about serving it, and the adults will love this dish, too.

BUTTERNUT MACARONI AND CHEESE instead!

GATHER

1 package (454 g) brown-rice or
   whole wheat macaroni*

1 teaspoon extra-virgin olive oil

¼ cup diced shallot or onion

1 clove garlic, crushed

4 cups cooked cubed butternut
   squash

1¼ cups almond milk**

½ cup plain Greek yogourt

2 teaspoons Dijon mustard

1 teaspoon prepared mustard

1 teaspoon low-sodium soy sauce

½ teaspoon nutmeg

½ teaspoon salt

¼ teaspoon pepper

3 tablespoons nutritional yeast

¾ cup shredded old white cheddar
   cheese

¼ cup light goat cheese

¼ cup grated Parmesan cheese

¼ cup breadcrumbs*

*For a gluten-free option, use brown-rice
   pasta and crumbs.

**Use cow's or soy milk to keep it nut-free.

MAKE

Cook pasta according to package directions, rinse and drain. Transfer to large casserole or baking dish.

Meanwhile, in small nonstick pan, heat oil over medium heat. Cook shallot until translucent, about 2 to 3 minutes.

In food processor or blender, combine shallot, garlic, squash, almond milk, yogourt, Dijon mustard, prepared mustard, soy sauce, nutmeg, salt, pepper and yeast and blend until smooth.

Transfer to large saucepan over medium heat. Stir in cheddar and goat cheese and cook, stirring, until cheese has melted and mixture is smooth. Pour over pasta, stirring to coat. Top with Parmesan and breadcrumbs. Bake in 350°F oven until topping is golden, about 25 minutes.

Serves 6.

VEGETARIAN OPTION

DAIRY-FREE OPTION

GLUTEN-FREE OPTION

NUT-FREE OPTION

No More
NUTELLA!

Nutella recently faced a court challenge of its claim to be "good for you." It lost the challenge because of the spread's high sugar content. Nutella is made, of course, from hazelnuts, so it's not school-friendly anyhow. Here's a nut-free, natural Nutella substitute that tastes great with sliced bananas on whole-grain bread.

SUNTELLA instead!

GATHER

1 cup sunflower seed butter

4 tablespoons cocoa powder

¼ cup (about) almond, soy or cow's milk*

¼ cup liquid honey

2 teaspoons vanilla extract

*For a nut-free option, use soy or cow's milk. For a dairy-free option, use almond or soy milk.

MAKE

In food processor, combine all ingredients and process until blended, thinning to spreadable consistency with more milk, if necessary.

Makes 48 portions.

"Please make that chocolate spread, Mom. It's so yummy!"
– Amelia, age 8

No More CANNED SOUP!

Such a delicious alternative to canned soup, this is one of my son Duncan's all-time favourites. Everyone eats it. It freezes well and is a perfect big-batch soup to make on the weekend. A hearty soup, it's chock full of protein, fibre, vitamins A, B and C, iron and folate. Serve it with crusty whole wheat bread.

DUNCAN'S FAMOUS SOUP instead!

GATHER

1 tablespoon olive or coconut oil

1 onion, chopped

3 cups chopped mushrooms

¾ cup pearl barley*

6 cups water

4 cups low-sodium vegetable stock

2 carrots, peeled and diced

1 large sweet potato, peeled and diced

2 bay leaves

¾ cup dried green lentils, picked over and rinsed

1 to 2 teaspoons sea salt

¼ teaspoon pepper

2 cups chopped kale or chard

Grated Asiago or Parmesan cheese (optional)

*For a gluten-free alternative, substitute brown rice.

MAKE

In stockpot, heat oil over medium heat. Sauté onion until softened. Stir in mushrooms and cook until softened, about 5 minutes. Stir in barley and cook, stirring, for 1 minute. Stir in water and stock. Increase heat to high, stir in carrots, sweet potato, bay leaves, lentils, half of the salt and the pepper and bring to a boil. Reduce heat and simmer, adding kale or chard after 30 minutes, until vegetables are tender, about 1 hour. Remove bay leaves. Taste soup and adjust salt, if necessary (saltiness will vary with brand of stock). Sprinkle with cheese, if desired.

Serves 8.

A Sneaky Trick that Works!

Why do we call this Duncan's Famous Soup, you ask? Simple. My son was never a soup lover. From an early age, his sister would slurp it back, but not him. One day, when he was five, I asked him if he wanted to help with dinner. He peeled the carrots, rinsed the lentils, added the bay leaves, measured the stock and stirred the mushrooms, then set the table with pride. At dinner, the rest of us raved about the soup, and I told him it was so delicious that from now on, it would be known as Duncan's Famous Soup. Helping to prepare the soup and being its namesake gave him ownership of the soup and motivated him to try it and — even better — to like it. I mean, you can't have a dish named after you that you don't like, right? Even a five-year-old gets that. From that day on, soup was in his repertoire, and his soup-lovin' mama was happy.

Duncan has a cousin named Jack, who is — in politically correct parlance — a highly selective eater. When Jack got wind of Duncan's Famous Soup, he wanted something named after him, too. I fed him my yummy sweet potato cake, and, when he asked for seconds, we renamed it Jack's Snack (page 117). Get creative and give your kids a stake in making and eating nutritious food. It works every time.

"Yum." (said with kale hanging out of mouth)
— Nolan, age 18 months

VEGETARIAN OPTION

DAIRY-FREE OPTION

GLUTEN-FREE OPTION

NUT-FREE OPTION

FREEZER-FRIENDLY

I have an onion-hater by the name of Georgia. She can spot an onion, of any variety, from a mile away. She is adept at manoeuvring around them in a soup, stew or stir-fry. I sat her down with a bowl of this "Cream" of Mushroom Soup after school one day, and asked her to be my tester. When she asked for more, I ladled it up and disclosed the secret ingredient: leeks, proud members of the onion family. After a little creative reasoning, she agreed that she didn't dislike onions quite as much as she had thought. "Cream" of Mushroom Soup has been a cold-weather staple in our house ever since, and onions seem to go down just a little easier for Georgia. Yukon Gold potatoes are my first choice for this, but any kind will do.

"CREAM" OF MUSHROOM SOUP instead!

GATHER

3 tablespoons virgin coconut oil

3 leeks (white and light green parts only), chopped

2 green onions, chopped

3 to 4 cloves garlic, crushed

6 cups chopped peeled potatoes

1½ cups chopped white mushrooms

4 cups low-sodium vegetable stock

2 cups water

¾ teaspoon nutmeg

¾ teaspoon salt

½ teaspoon ground dried thyme

¼ teaspoon pepper

MAKE

In stockpot, heat oil over medium heat. Sauté leeks and onions until softened, about 10 minutes.

Stir in remaining ingredients and bring to a boil. Reduce heat and simmer until potatoes are fork-tender, about 30 minutes.

Remove from heat and let cool slightly. With immersion blender (or in batches in food processor), purée until smooth.

Serves 9.

No More
PLASTIC CHEESE!

VEGETARIAN OPTION

NUT-FREE OPTION

"Healthing it up" when it comes to grilled cheese sandwiches is simple. Switch the white bread with whole wheat, processed cheese with real white cheddar, and margarine with a spritz of olive oil, and you've already significantly boosted the nutrition in this lunch staple. Add thin slices of pear, apple or tomato, or a smear of avocado, and you've taken this sandwich up another notch.

Grill this baby in a sandwich press to reduce the fat added in cooking, and you've got yourself a real, good-for-you, grilled cheese.

GOOD-FOR-YOU GRILLED CHEESE instead!

GATHER

½ teaspoon extra-virgin olive oil

2 slices whole wheat bread

Enough thinly sliced white cheddar cheese to cover bread slice

Thinly sliced fruit, tomato or avocado (optional), for extra toppings

MAKE

Brush oil evenly over 1 side of each bread slice. Place oiled side of 1 slice on panini press, grill or skillet over medium heat. Top with cheddar and extra toppings, if desired, and sandwich with second slice, oil side up. Cook (turning once if using grill or skillet) until bread is golden brown and cheese has melted.

Serves 1.

Cheesy but True

This surprises many of the parents I meet: cheddar cheese is not naturally orange. Milk is white, so any orange cheese has had colour added to it and, usually, that colouring isn't natural. Here's another interesting fact: white cheddar cheese is available. One of the first and easiest changes you can make in your quest to "get real" is to switch to white cheddar. One caution: Remarkably, I have also come across white cheese with artificial colour listed as an ingredient on the label.

No More
FROZEN PIZZAS!

Superquick, spelt thin-crust pizza is always a crowd-pleaser for play dates at our house. Top the crust with homemade or jarred natural tomato sauce, Dillyicious Sauce (page 75) or Spinach Pesto Sauce (page 74), loads of chopped veggies and a cup or so of shredded skim mozzarella or crumbled feta cheese. My family's favourite combo is pesto sauce topped with chopped spinach, sliced tomatoes, mushrooms, olives and black beans.

EASY PIZZA CRUST *instead!*

GATHER

1 clove garlic, crushed

2 cups (about) spelt flour

1½ teaspoons quick-rising (instant)
    dry yeast

1 teaspoon oregano

1 teaspoon basil

½ teaspoon sea salt

2/3 cup warm water

1 tablespoon liquid honey

1 tablespoon extra-virgin olive oil

Toppings as desired

MAKE

In large bowl, whisk together garlic, flour, yeast, oregano, basil and salt. Stir in water, honey and oil until blended and dough forms ball. Cover with tea towel, transfer to stovetop, turning on oven to 425°F and opening oven door just a crack, and let rise for about 10 minutes. Close oven door and transfer dough to well-floured surface.

Knead dough, adding more flour if necessary to prevent sticking, for about 3 minutes. Punch down into flat disc, then roll into 12-inch circle. Transfer to lightly oiled 12-inch pan, stretching dough to shape slightly raised rim. Add toppings and bake at 425°F until crust is crisp and browned, about 18 to 20 minutes.

Dough can be frozen raw, then defrosted for use on a busy weeknight. Just let it rise once defrosted, as per instructions, above, before rolling out.

Serves 5.

"This pizza is delicious. I would eat it every day if I could!"
— Luke, age 9

Start with this basic recipe, then add whatever veggies and other healthy toppings your family will enjoy. Remember that most deli meats contain nitrites. These can combine with amino acids to produce carcinogenic nitrosamines in our digestive tracts, so check labels carefully before including these meats as toppings or choose a vegetarian protein alternative.

EASY PITA PIZZAS *instead!*

GATHER

4 small whole wheat (or 80% whole wheat) pitas

1 cup organic spaghetti sauce

1 cup chopped sliced mushrooms

1 cup finely chopped baby spinach

½ cup black or white beans, rinsed and drained

Fresh or dried oregano and basil to taste

1 cup shredded skim mozzarella cheese

MAKE

With spoon, spread each pita with one-quarter of the spaghetti sauce, then top with one-quarter of the mushrooms, spinach and beans. Evenly sprinkle each with oregano and basil, to taste, and one-quarter of the cheese.

Bake in 400°F oven until crust is crisp and cheese has melted, 8 to 10 minutes.

Serves 4.

"These are yummy and I love it when Mommy makes an extra for my lunchbox the next day!"
— Jasmine, age 6

The Winning Combination

Remember, while kids get most of their energy from carbohydrates, children need more than just grains (even the whole kind) to meet their nutritional needs.

Kids need other carbohydrates, such as those found in vegetables and fruit, to ensure they are getting a wide variety of vitamins and minerals. They also need good-quality proteins (such as those found in lean meat, eggs and beans) to build their growing bodies and beneficial fats from plant sources for their brain development and cell health. The best lunch includes a little protein and healthy fat, along with good carbs in the form of veggies, fruit and whole grains. If you pack their lunches with this balance in mind, your kids will benefit from a slower release of sugar into their bloodstreams during the afternoon, since protein and fat take longer to digest than carbs alone. This should help them focus and learn. As an added bonus, their teachers will love you!

No More
LUNCHABLES!

VEGETARIAN OPTION

NUT-FREE OPTION

Who needs all those nitrates and salt! Assemble your own deli-icious school lunches. Customize them — balancing protein, healthy fat and complex carbs (see The Winning Combination sidebar, page 50). Most bean dips, such as Yummus Hummus (page 92) and Double Dip (page 92) are good sources of both protein and healthy fat. Use plain Greek yogourt in your Tasty Tzatziki (page 97) and add another boost of protein. Give the Asiago and Garlic Pita Chips (page 109) a try and throw in some sliced or shredded vegetables, which are energy-filled complex carbs!

BASIC LUNCHBOX instead!

GATHER

1 hardcooked egg

Cubed skim mozzarella cheese

Whole wheat crackers such as
  Free-Range Goldfish (page 100)

Sliced apples and raisins

Sliced cucumbers and carrot sticks

MAKE

Divide these ingredients among several small containers or arrange in bento-style lunch box. Add a refillable bottle of water and you have a lunch that's really lunchable!

Serves 1.

LATIN LUNCHBOX *instead!*

GATHER

Free-Range Goldfish (page 100)

½ cup cubed precooked chicken
breast

2 tablespoons Holy "Guadamame"
(page 93)

2 tablespoons Double Dip (page 92)

Sliced veggies to dip

Sliced fruit, natural applesauce or
berries

MAKE

Divide these ingredients among several small containers or
arrange in bento-style lunch box. Add a refillable bottle of
water and you have a lunch that's really lunchable!

Serves 1.

MIDDLE EASTERN LUNCHBOX *instead!*

GATHER

Asiago and Garlic Pita Chips (page
109)

2 tablespoons Yummus Hummus
(page 92)

2 tablespoons Tasty Tzatziki (page 97)

¼ cup Crunchy Chickpeas
(page 110)

Sliced veggies to dip

Sliced fruit, natural applesauce
or berries

MAKE

Divide these ingredients among several small containers or
arrange in bento-style lunch box. Add a refillable bottle of
water and you have a lunch that's really lunchable!

Serves 1.

No More
PASTA FROM A CAN!

This easy whole-grain alternative to kids' canned pasta contains tomatoes, sweet potatoes and carrots for added veggie power. A big hit with my kids, this soup is part of their lunches most weeks.

HOMEMADE ALPHABET SOUP *instead!*

GATHER

1 cup uncooked whole wheat
  alphabet pasta

1½ teaspoons coconut oil

1 clove garlic, crushed

½ onion, finely diced

2 cups grated carrots

1 cup grated sweet potatoes

1 can or jar (28 ounces) crushed
  tomatoes

1 cup low-sodium vegetable stock

1 cup water

1 tablespoon liquid honey

1 tablespoon low-sodium soy sauce

2 teaspoons apple cider vinegar

1 teaspoon dried basil, or 1
  tablespoon fresh

1 teaspoon dried oregano, or 1
  tablespoon fresh

¾ teaspoon sea salt

¼ teaspoon pepper

½ cup grated Asiago cheese

MAKE

Cook pasta according to package directions. Drain and set aside.

Meanwhile, in stockpot or Dutch oven, heat oil over medium heat. Cook garlic, onion, carrots and sweet potatoes, stirring, until softened, 3 to 5 minutes. Stir in tomatoes, stock, water, honey, soy sauce, vinegar, basil, oregano, salt and pepper. Increase heat and bring to a boil. Reduce heat, cover and simmer, stirring occasionally, until vegetables are tender, 10 to 15 minutes. Remove from heat. With immersion blender (or in batches in food processor), blend until smooth. Stir in pasta and cheese. Return to heat and cook until mixture is heated through and cheese has melted.

Serves 8.

REAL DINNERS

Family dinners are important. They provide an opportunity for families to reconnect at the end of each day, as well as an opportunity to model healthy lifelong eating habits. If we include our children in the food preparation, we can share some positive education while we have an engaged and captive audience. Another bonus: A recent UK study found that children eat more fruits and vegetables when families sit down and eat together, and another study suggests children in these types of families may also have a lowered risk of becoming overweight. For many of us, eating together may not be possible every night, but, for all the above reasons, with a little planning and effort, we can make it happen most nights.

Finding simple, reliable and healthy recipes is key to planning your dinners in advance, taking into account the timing of your family's daily activities. The recipes in this chapter should help get you started, and the meal-planning tips in the Introduction will get you organized.

You can do it!

Natural Healers

Certain foods contain powerful natural substances that can, for example, decrease inflammation, support immunity, help regulate blood sugar or act as antibacterials and antifungals. Whenever I can, I try to include these foods in my recipes and cooking. For example, turmeric, which I use in my curries, contains a substance called curcumin, which is a powerful anti-inflammatory. Cinnamon, which I try to include in as many breakfasts and baked recipes as possible, can help to regulate blood sugar. Garlic and onions, which are featured in most of my savoury recipes, can help your body strengthen its immunity and fight bacteria. Coconut oil is a natural anti-inflammatory and antifungal food. Fruits and vegetables rich in antioxidants — such as vitamins A, C, E and the mineral selenium — can help repair cell damage. Most of the kids I know love trivia. Why not teach your kids some fun facts about the powers of real food? You might be amazed at how a little knowledge makes a big difference to their tastes and habits.

"This soup tastes better than the soup at a Chinese restaurant."
— Kellyn, age 12

No More
INSTANT NOODLES!

This is the ultimate chicken noodle soup for whatever ails you. It contains garlic, ginger and onions, three of the best natural cold-fighters and anti-inflammatories out there, dark leafy greens for a shot of energy and a sweet sesame flavour that everyone will love. Traditional soba noodles are made of buckwheat, a non-gluten grain that is high in fibre and nutrients. Available in the natural food section of most grocery stores and at health food stores, these hearty noodles make this soup a filling and comforting meal. Turns out, some soup is good food.

MAMA'S CHICKEN SOBA SOUP instead!

GATHER

8 ounces (½ pound) uncooked soba noodles, 100% buckwheat

1 teaspoon extra-virgin olive oil

3 cloves garlic, crushed

1 large carrot, peeled and thinly sliced

1 large stalk celery, thinly sliced

½ cup chopped onion

4 cups low-sodium chicken stock*

4 cups water

1 tablespoon grated fresh ginger

¼ teaspoon sea salt

¼ teaspoon pepper

1 boneless, skinless, uncooked chicken breast, thinly sliced, then cut in 1-inch strips*

2 cups fresh spinach, sliced in thin ribbons

¼ cup lime juice (juice of about 1 small lime)

2 teaspoons toasted sesame oil

1 tablespoon low-sodium soy sauce

3 green onions, thinly sliced

MAKE

Cook noodles according to package directions. Drain and set aside.

Meanwhile, in stockpot or Dutch oven, heat olive oil over medium heat. Cook garlic, carrots, celery and onion, adding a little of the stock, if necessary, to prevent browning, until softened.

Stir in stock, water, ginger, salt and pepper. Increase heat and bring to a boil. Stir in chicken, reduce heat and simmer until chicken strips are opaque, about 3 minutes. Stir in spinach, lime juice, sesame oil and soy sauce and cook until spinach is bright green, 1 or 2 minutes. Remove from heat and stir in noodles. Garnish with green onions (and an extra dose of mama love).

*For a vegan version, use vegetable stock and replace chicken with 1 cup shelled edamame beans or cubed firm tofu.

Serves 6 to 7

No More
INSTANT SIDES!

My son Duncan loves the taste of alfredo sauce. It's usually either made from a package or with heavy cream, butter and cheese, and is often also very high in sodium, so I wasn't keen to include it on our family's dinner roster. Because Duncan is nothing if not persistent, I eventually came up with a healthier, lower-dairy version that's "nothing to be alfredo"! Both of my kids love it and regularly enjoy the leftovers at school for lunch. Filling and tasty, this dish is a great way to load up on carbs before a practice or a big game!

EASY CHICKEN ALFREDO BAKE instead!

GATHER

1 pound whole wheat penne or
   rotini*

2 cups fresh broccoli florets

1 teaspoon extra-virgin olive oil

3 cloves garlic, crushed

¾ cup chopped onion

Juice of 1 lemon

1 block (340 g) silken tofu

1 cup unsweetened almond milk**

½ cup grated Asiago or Parmesan
   cheese

2 tablespoons nutritional yeast

½ teaspoon salt

¼ teaspoon pepper

1 cooked boneless skinless chicken
   breast, cubed

¼ cup panko breadcrumbs*

*For a gluten-free recipe, use brown-rice
   pasta and brown-rice crumbs.

**Use cow's or soy milk to keep nut-free.

MAKE

In large pot of boiling salted water, cook pasta and broccoli until tender. Drain, transfer to baking dish and set aside.

Meanwhile, in small saucepan over medium heat, heat oil. Sauté garlic and onion until softened.

In food processor or blender, combine garlic mixture, lemon juice, tofu, milk, cheese, yeast, salt and pepper and blend until smooth. Stir into pasta mixture along with chicken to coat and combine.

Sprinkle with breadcrumbs and bake in 350°F oven until golden and heated through, about 20 minutes.

Tip: For a different flavour, blend one jar of roasted sweet red peppers into the sauce!

Serves 8.

No More
MEATBALL SUB!

VEGETARIAN OPTION

GLUTEN-FREE OPTION

FREEZER-FRIENDLY

Surprisingly like meat in texture and taste, these also freeze very well. Simmer them in your favourite sweet-and-sour or marinara marinade and no one will know they are meatless!
For a meaty alternative, try my yummy Tasty Turkey Sliders or Meatballs (page 64).

WALNUT MEATBALLS *instead!*

GATHER

2 cloves garlic

2 cups large-flake rolled oats*

½ cup broken walnuts

½ cup raw pumpkin seeds

1 cup low-fat ricotta cheese

½ cup egg whites

½ cup chopped onion

¼ cup chopped parsley

¼ cup grated Parmesan cheese

3 tablespoons nutritional yeast

1 teaspoon dried basil

1 teaspoon dried oregano

1 cup low-sodium vegetable stock

1 cup water

*To ensure recipe is gluten-free, use certified gluten-free oats, as cross-contamination can occur in processing.

MAKE

In food processor, combine garlic, oats, walnuts and pumpkin seeds and process until blended and smooth. Transfer to large bowl. Stir in ricotta, egg whites, onion, parsley, Parmesan, yeast, basil and oregano.

With hands, shape into about 30 one-inch balls and transfer to nonstick baking sheet.

Bake in 400°F oven, turning once halfway through, for 20 minutes.

Transfer to Dutch oven or roasting pan. In large glass measure, combine stock and water, then pour over meatballs, adding more water, if necessary, to almost cover meatballs. Reduce heat to 325°F. Cover and bake for 45 minutes.

With slotted spoon or tongs, remove from liquid to serve.

Tip: Instead of cooking meatballs in stock mixture for the last 45 minutes of baking, cover with marinara or other sauce.

Serves 6 to 8.

No More
INSTANT SIDES!

Another quick and delicious alternative to traditional alfredo, this dairy-free dish is amazingly creamy and comforting. A huge hit, it's gobbled up by kids, kale and all!

Tofu is an extremely versatile ingredient and simple to cook with, but many people I meet are either afraid of the unknown or don't know what to do with tofu. Choose organic tofu and soy products when they're available (otherwise the soy may be genetically modified). Use firm or extra-firm tofu for this recipe; it's easy to cut and holds its form. Cooked, cubed chicken can easily be substituted in the place of tofu and tastes equally delicious.

PEANUT BUTTER PASTA WITH KALE *instead!*

GATHER

1 package (454 g) whole wheat
   pasta*

1 package (454 g) organic firm or
   extra-firm tofu

½ cup (about) water

¼ cup low-sodium soy sauce

3 tablespoons natural peanut butter
   or almond butter

1 tablespoon apple cider vinegar

1 teaspoon coconut oil

1 teaspoon sesame oil (optional)

2 cloves garlic, crushed

4 cups destemmed chopped kale or
   spinach, or 2 cups broccoli florets
   and 2 cups destemmed chopped
   kale or spinach

2 tablespoons black or white
   sesame seeds (optional)

*For a gluten-free version, use
   brown-rice pasta.

MAKE

Cook pasta according to package directions. Drain, set aside and keep warm.

Meanwhile, with paper towel, pat tofu dry. Cut into 1-inch slices, then into cubes.

In large glass measuring cup, whisk together water, soy sauce, peanut butter and vinegar until blended into a sauce.

In large skillet or wok, heat coconut oil and sesame oil, if desired, over medium heat. Sauté garlic until fragrant, about 1 minute. Stir in tofu and cook, stirring, until golden. Gently toss in kale and/or spinach (and broccoli, if desired) and cook, stirring, until wilted. Stir in sauce and cook until thickened. Reduce heat and cook until heated through, adding more water if sauce gets too thick. Top with sesame seeds, if desired, and serve over pasta.

Serves 5 to 6.

Happier at Home

What's the best thing about a McDonald's Happy Meal? The creative packaging, of course! For your homemade "Happier Meals," decorate a paper bag or other fun food container, and throw in a toy from the dollar store or a funny personalized note, then choose one of these real-food options:

Coconut Pecan Crusted Nuggets with Honey Mustard Dip (page 63) and Busy Bee Dip (page 98), Tasty Turkey Sliders or Meatballs (page 64) or Sesame Mushroom Burgers (page 66) on a small whole wheat bun or tucked into a pita half, Good-for-You Grilled Cheese (page 47), serving of Sweet Potato Fries (page 84) or Wedges (page 73), sliced apple with Little Dipper sauce (page 94), or make a yogourt parfait with ½ cup plain Greek yogourt, 1 teaspoon liquid honey and 1 tablespoon Basic Birkenstock Granola (page 30). Include a drink container filled with water, milk or a milk alternative or some Basic Family Smoothie (page 36).

No More
CHICKEN NUGGETS!

VEGETARIAN
OPTION

GLUTEN-FREE
OPTION

Here are some healthier, tasty ways to prepare nuggets and burgers at home, with ingredients you can pronounce and feel happy about serving.

COCONUT PECAN CRUSTED NUGGETS WITH HONEY MUSTARD DIP *instead!*

GATHER

1 block (454 g) firm or extra-firm
   organic tofu or 1 large boneless
   skinless chicken breast

2/3 cup water

2 tablespoons low-sodium soy sauce

1 tablespoon prepared mustard

Grated zest and juice of 1 lime

1/2 cup large-flake rolled oats*

2 tablespoons ground flaxseed

2 tablespoons pecans

1/4 teaspoon garlic powder

1/8 teaspoon salt

1/8 teaspoon pepper

1/4 cup unsweetened shredded
   coconut

1/4 cup liquid egg whites

Busy Bee Dip (page 98)

*To ensure recipe is gluten-free,
   use certified gluten-free oats, as
   cross-contamination can occur in
   processing.

MAKE

With paper towel, pat tofu dry. Slice into 8 slabs, then cut each slab into 4 cubes (or cut chicken into 2-inch cubes).

In baking dish, whisk together water, soy sauce, mustard and lime juice. Stir in tofu or chicken to coat. (For an even more flavourful nugget, let tofu or chicken marinate for a few hours — or even overnight — in the refrigerator.)

In food processor, combine oats, flaxseed, pecans, garlic powder, salt and pepper and pulse until mixture resembles coarse flour. Add lime zest and coconut and pulse until combined. Evenly spread mixture over dinner plate.

Pour egg whites into small bowl. One cube at a time, dip tofu or chicken into egg whites, then roll in oat mixture to coat, and transfer to nonstick baking sheet.

Bake in 350°F oven, gently turning after 15 minutes, for 25 to 30 minutes. (Or, for chicken, until cooked through.) Serve with dip.

Serves 6.

No More
MEATBALL SUB!

These delicious sliders or meatballs (call them whatever you want) freeze well. Quick to defrost, they can be added to soups and sauces or used in mini-burgers, sandwiches and subs — with sliced veggies on top — for a satisfying and real fast-food dinner. This recipe also makes great summertime turkey burgers for the grill!

TASTY TURKEY SLIDERS
OR MEATBALLS *instead!*

GATHER

2 pounds extra-lean ground turkey

2 cups fresh, finely chopped spinach

¾ cup chopped onion

2 green onions, sliced

3 cloves garlic, crushed

2 large eggs

½ cup grated Parmesan cheese

½ cup ground flaxseed

1 teaspoon dried sage

½ teaspoon dried marjoram

½ teaspoon dried thyme

½ teaspoon pepper

¾ cup large-flake rolled oats*

*To ensure recipe is gluten-free, use certified gluten-free oats, as cross-contamination can occur in processing.

MAKE

In large bowl, combine all ingredients, adding the rolled oats last. Let stand for 5 minutes.

With hands, shape into about 20 small patties (or 40 meatballs) and transfer to nonstick baking sheet.

Bake in 350°F oven until golden, about 20 minutes.

Serves 10.

"Delish!"

— Georgia, age 8

No More
TAKEOUT BURGERS!

Yummo. This was a last-minute creation for a summertime book-club dinner. It was gorgeous outside and way too hot in my kitchen, so I wanted to grill the whole meal but didn't want to serve meat or my usual veggie burgers. These pair up nicely with Roasted Veggie Penne Salad (page 87). Beautiful!

PORTOBELLOS WITH HERBED GOAT CHEESE AND SPINACH *instead!*

GATHER

3 tablespoons balsamic vinegar, divided

3 tablespoons extra-virgin olive oil, divided

8 large portobello mushrooms, stems removed

3 cups fresh, finely chopped spinach

2 tablespoons fresh, finely chopped rosemary

2 cloves garlic, crushed

1 package (140 g) goat cheese, crumbled

2 tablespoons grated Asiago cheese

MAKE

In small bowl, stir together 2 tablespoons each balsamic oil and olive oil. Brush oil mixture all over each mushroom and transfer, cap up, to BBQ grill pan.

Grill until tender, 10 to 15 minutes. Meanwhile, in saucepan, heat remaining balsamic oil and olive oil over medium heat. Toss in spinach, rosemary and garlic to coat and cook, stirring, until spinach has wilted. Transfer to small bowl and toss in goat cheese.

Invert mushrooms on grill pan. Top each with 1 tablespoon of the spinach mixture and sprinkle with Asiago. Grill until heated through and cheese has melted.

Serves 8.

These are hearty enough to satisfy any beef lover! You can replace the carrots with just about any shredded veggie.

SESAME MUSHROOM BURGERS *instead!*

GATHER

2 large eggs

1 pound firm organic tofu

1½ cups grated carrots

½ cup large-flake rolled oats*

½ cup sliced mushrooms

½ cup pumpkin seeds

¼ cup sunflower seeds

¼ cup sesame seeds

2 tablespoons reduced-sodium soy
   sauce

1½ tablespoons Dijon mustard

1 tablespoon toasted sesame oil

¼ teaspoon sea salt

1 teaspoon olive or coconut oil

*To ensure recipe is gluten-free,
   use certified gluten-free oats, as
   cross-contamination can occur in
   processing.

MAKE

In food processor, combine eggs, tofu, carrots, oats, mushrooms, pumpkin seeds, sunflower seeds, sesame seeds, soy sauce, mustard, sesame oil and salt and pulse, scraping down side, until combined. Shape into 8 patties (or 16 mini-burgers).

In cast-iron skillet, heat olive or coconut oil over medium heat. Cook patties, turning once halfway through, until browned and heated through, about 10 minutes (or grill on lightly greased BBQ tray, turning once).

Burgers can be frozen after cooking.

Serves 8.

No More
BURRITO KITS!

VEGETARIAN OPTION

DAIRY-FREE OPTION

GLUTEN-FREE OPTION

NUT-FREE OPTION

FREEZER-FRIENDLY

Making and seasoning your own burritos is easy and allows you to control the ingredients and keep them junk-free. I'm including my Sweet Potato Burritos, which are very popular with big and little people, to get you started. Filling and delicious, these burritos provide loads of beta carotene, potassium, iron, protein and fibre. You can also prepare this in advance. Freeze the burritos and sauce separately, then defrost, combine and heat through for a quick weeknight meal.

SWEET POTATO BURRITOS WITH ENCHILADA SAUCE instead!

FOR BURRITOS: GATHER

1 teaspoon extra-virgin olive oil

2 large carrots, peeled and grated

1 clove garlic, crushed

2 cups chopped spinach

2 cups chopped mushrooms

1 teaspoon ground cumin

10 large 100% whole wheat tortillas*

1 can (425 g) low-fat refried beans

2 large sweet potatoes, cooked and mashed

1 cup shredded part-skim mozzarella cheese**

1 can (540 g) black beans (or about 1 cup fresh, cooked), rinsed and drained

*For gluten-free burritos, use brown-rice or organic corn tortillas.

**For dairy-free, vegan burritos, use shredded vegan cheese.

MAKE

In skillet, heat oil over medium heat. Stir in carrots, garlic, spinach, mushrooms and cumin and sauté until mushrooms have softened. Set aside. On work surface, lay tortillas flat. Smear about 2 tablespoons of the refried beans down centre of each. Repeat with about ¼ cup of the sweet potatoes and sprinkle with about 2 tablespoons of cheese. Top each with about ¼ cup of the carrot mixture and about 2 tablespoons of the black beans. Wrap up each, burrito-style (to freeze, wrap separately with plastic wrap, then transfer to freezer bag).

FOR SAUCE: GATHER

2 tablespoons extra-virgin olive oil

1½ tablespoons whole wheat flour***

1 tablespoon chili powder

1 can (156 g) tomato paste

1 clove garlic, crushed

1½ cups water

¼ teaspoon ground cumin

¼ teaspoon onion powder

***For a gluten-free sauce, use brown-rice flour.

MAKE

In skillet, heat oil over medium heat. Stir in flour and chili powder, reduce heat to low and cook, stirring, until golden brown. Stir in remaining ingredients until blended and cook until thickened, about 10 minutes (to freeze, let cool and transfer to airtight container).

ASSEMBLE

In glass baking dish lightly sprayed with olive oil, arrange burritos, top with sauce and bake in 350°F oven for 15 to 20 minutes.

Tip: Sprinkle on even more grated cheese before baking, if you like.

Serves 10.

No More
MSG-LADEN TAKEOUT!

Who needs takeout when you can whip these up! The first time I served them, they provoked a lively discussion about Buddha and karma. My kids loved the yummy sauce and the possibility that they could achieve both good karma and red pee by eating these (grated beets are a key ingredient). When you stir-fry the veggies, remember not to overcook — you'll preserve more of their nutrients and enzymes, and crunchy tastes better. You can make the sauce in advance, then give it a shake to recombine before serving. About an hour before you prep the veggies and sauce, throw a couple of cups of brown rice into the rice cooker to complete your dinner. I think you'll agree this sauce is crazily addictive! Namaste!

KARMIC BUDDHA BOWLS instead!

GATHER

1 clove garlic, crushed

½ cup water

¼ cup extra-virgin olive oil

¼ cup nutritional yeast

¼ cup low-sodium soy sauce

¼ cup apple cider vinegar

2 tablespoons tahini

2 cups grated carrots (about 4 large)

2 cups grated beets (about 3 to 4)

2 cups grated red or green cabbage

2 teaspoons coconut oil

2 cups cubed firm organic tofu

Beet greens, chopped

1 to 2 cups chopped spinach, kale,
   bok choy or chard

2 cups cooked brown rice

MAKE

In food processor, combine garlic, water, olive oil, yeast, soy sauce, vinegar and tahini and blend until smooth. Set aside. In food processor fitted with grater attachment (or with box grater), grate carrots, beets and cabbage. Set aside.

In wok, heat coconut oil over medium heat. Stir-fry tofu until golden. With slotted spoon, remove tofu and set aside.

In wok, stir-fry carrots, beets, cabbage, beet greens and spinach until slightly softened. Into each of 6 serving bowls, spoon ⅓ cup rice, evenly divide veggie mixture overtop and sprinkle with tofu. Top each with about ¼ cup sauce.

The sauce, tofu, steamed shredded veggies and brown rice can be frozen separately, or as pre-assembled bowls for an easy grab-and-go lunch or dinner.

Serves 6.

No More
PREPARED SAUCES!

So healthy and easy, this curry is also free of gluten and dairy products. It's not too spicy so it works for the whole family — the honey and coconut milk add sweetness to this mild dish. You can substitute in virtually any veggies you have in the fridge — mushrooms, broccoli, potatoes, peas and green beans are all great. I prefer to buy the light version of coconut milk, but you can also use standard coconut milk. My children love this for supper, spooned over brown rice or pasta. Either quinoa or brown rice will make this a gluten-free meal.

ANY VEGGIE COCONUT CURRY *instead!*

GATHER

1 teaspoon coconut oil

1 small onion, chopped

4 cloves garlic, crushed

3 large carrots, chopped or thinly
   sliced

½ cup low-sodium vegetable stock

1½ tablespoons curry powder

1 teaspoon ground cumin

½ teaspoon turmeric

¼ teaspoon sea salt

2 large tomatoes, coarsely chopped

2 cups chopped dark leafy greens
   such as Swiss chard, spinach or kale

1 cup diced peeled sweet potato

1 cup shelled edamame beans

1 can (14 ounce) chickpeas, rinsed
   and drained

1 can (398 g) light coconut milk

2 tablespoons liquid honey

MAKE

In stockpot or Dutch oven, melt coconut oil over medium heat. Sauté onions, garlic and carrots until onions are translucent (add a few spoonfuls of stock, if necessary, to prevent sticking). Stir in curry powder, cumin, turmeric and salt and cook, stirring frequently, for 2 to 4 minutes. Stir in tomatoes, greens, sweet potato, edamame, chickpeas, coconut milk and honey and bring to a low boil. Reduce heat to medium-low, cover and simmer, stirring occasionally, until sweet potato is fork-tender, 15 to 20 minutes (if desired, let cool, transfer to airtight container and refrigerate for up to 3 days; reheat before serving).

Serves 10.

No More
INSTANT CHILI!

Healthy homemade chili is one of the easiest kid-friendly dinners to throw together in a hurry and it's so much healthier than takeout! My niece Stella (she's two) says this is her favourite. It's my favourite, too. It's impossible to mess up and freezes well. You can use peppers or mushrooms — or any other lonely veggies in your crisper — instead of the carrots. You can also substitute chopped fresh tomatoes for the canned. If the chili gets too thick as it cooks, just add a little more stock or water. This is yummy with a handful of baked organic tortilla chips on the side, or served over brown rice!

SIMPLE VEGGIE CHILI instead!

GATHER

2 tablespoons extra-virgin olive oil

4 cloves garlic, crushed or chopped

1 yellow onion, chopped

2 cups peeled and chopped carrots (about 3 large)

2 cups peeled and cubed sweet potato (about 1 large)

1 can (28 ounce) no-salt–added crushed tomatoes

1 can (14 ounce) black beans, rinsed and drained

1 can (14 ounce) kidney beans, rinsed and drained

2 cups low-sodium vegetable stock

1 cup chickpeas or white beans, rinsed and drained (or ½ of a 454 g block crumbled organic tofu)

1 to 2 tablespoons chili powder

1 tablespoon ground cumin

1 teaspoon dried dill

1 teaspoon sea salt

Plain Greek yogourt (optional)

MAKE

In stockpot or Dutch oven, heat oil over medium heat. Sauté garlic, onion, carrots and sweet potato until softened, 3 to 5 minutes. Stir in tomatoes, black beans, kidney beans, stock and chickpeas. Stir in chili powder to taste, cumin, dill and salt.

Reduce heat and simmer for 15 to 20 minutes. Top individual servings with yogourt, if desired.

Serves 10.

"More. More." (his mother's interpretation of baby sign language)
— Owen, age 1

DAIRY-FREE OPTION

GLUTEN-FREE OPTION

NUT-FREE OPTION

FREEZER-FRIENDLY

No More
TAKE-OUT CHICKEN!

If you've never done it, try roasting your own whole chicken. You'll be surprised at how economical and straightforward it is and so much healthier than at a restaurant. If you cook it on the weekend, you can carve it up and use it for sandwiches during the week or freeze some for a later date. It's a lot healthier than nitrite- and sodium-laden deli meat.

This recipe makes chicken so moist and flavourful that you won't need a too-salty dipping sauce. While you're at it, you might as well roast some Potato Wedges (page 73)! Quarter Chicken Dinners all around!

THIS CHALET CHICKEN *instead!*

GATHER

1 clove garlic, crushed

1 teaspoon melted coconut oil

1 teaspoon poultry seasoning

¼ teaspoon salt

3½ pound whole roasting chicken

1 lemon or lime, quartered

MAKE

In small bowl, stir together garlic, oil, poultry seasoning and salt. With your fingers, loosen skin on chicken breast and thighs. Rub garlic mixture evenly under skin. Place lemon or lime into cavity. Transfer chicken, breast side up, to rack in roasting pan. Bake in 400°F oven, until meat thermometer inserted in thigh (do not touch bone) registers 180°F, about 1 hour 10 minutes. Let stand for 10 minutes. Remove lemon or lime and skin, then carve.

Roasted chicken can be sliced once cool, then frozen.

Serves 6.

When you're roasting a chicken, throw these into the oven for the last 35 minutes of cooking time, then everything will be ready at the same time (roast the potatoes on the lowest rack, under the chicken pan).

GARLIC AND ROSEMARY POTATO WEDGES

GATHER

1 clove garlic, crushed

2 teaspoons crumbled dried rosemary

½ tablespoons melted coconut oil

⅛ teaspoon sea salt

4 unpeeled russet potatoes, scrubbed, quartered and cut in wedges

MAKE

In large bowl, stir together garlic, rosemary, oil and salt. Toss in potatoes to coat. Transfer to nonstick baking sheet. Bake in 400°F oven, turning after 20 minutes, for 35 minutes.

Serves 6.

VEGAN OPTION

DAIRY-FREE OPTION

GLUTEN-FREE OPTION

NUT-FREE OPTION

No More
JARRED SPAGHETTI SAUCE!

A cube of Spinach Pesto Sauce can save your life on a busy weeknight! One cube thaws quickly and it's enough to dress two or three fish fillets or chicken breasts before they are baked or grilled and enough to flavour a family-size pot of pasta. One cube makes a great base for salad dressing, excellent over grilled veggies or as a topping in a crusty sandwich. This recipe also makes enough sauce for three pizzas. Adjust the basil and garlic to your liking, and omit the cheese if you are avoiding dairy foods.

SPINACH PESTO SAUCE *instead!*

GATHER

3 cloves garlic

2 cups packed fresh spinach

½ cup packed fresh basil

⅓ cup pine nuts, walnuts or pecans

3 tablespoons grated Parmesan or
    Asiago cheese

½ teaspoon pepper

¼ cup extra-virgin olive oil

MAKE

In blender or food processor, combine garlic, spinach, basil, nuts, cheese and pepper. Slowly pouring in oil, blend until a paste forms (transfer to airtight container and refrigerate for up to 1 week).

Serves 6 to 8 (over pasta).

"?Mas, Mama?"
— Alma, age 2 and
learning Spanish

Put whole wheat pasta on to boil, then whip up this sauce in a food processor in 5 minutes — a gourmet, family-friendly, fast food treat! It only takes a few spoonfuls to dress a family-size portion of pasta. The sauce is also perfect as a healthy pizza topping. You can sprinkle each serving with more grated cheese. And don't forget to let your family in on the secret healthy ingredients: edamame and kale.

DILLYICIOUS SAUCE *instead!*

GATHER

1 small shallot

1 clove garlic, crushed

Juice of half a lemon

1 cup frozen edamame or green
 peas or combination (thawed)

1 cup chopped kale

½ cup grated Asiago or Parmesan
 cheese

1 teaspoon dried dill

¼ teaspoon salt

¼ cup extra-virgin olive oil

MAKE

In food processor, chop shallot. Add garlic, lemon juice, edamame, kale, cheese, dill and salt and blend. Slowly pouring in oil, blend until smooth.

Serves 4 to 6 (over pasta).

No More
JARRED SPAGHETTI!

Whenever my kids get excited about a new healthy recipe, I let them name it. This gives them ownership and ensures that they will eat it — no complaints — the next time I serve it. All to say: I know it's a ridiculous name, but there's a good reason behind it! This pasta alternative arose because I needed something yummy to make with all the spaghetti squash and shallots we found in our farm-share box. It's really easy to throw together, but just make sure you allow 35 minutes or so to prebake the squash, and about 20 minutes to bake the casserole.

YUMMY SQUASHGHETTI BAKE instead!

GATHER

1 spaghetti squash, halved
  lengthwise

1½ tablespoons extra-virgin olive oil

1 large shallot or white onion,
  finely chopped

3 tomatoes, chopped

1 clove garlic, crushed

3 tablespoons sliced black or
  green olives

2 tablespoons chopped fresh
  basil (or 2 teaspoons dried)

¾ cup diced or crumbled light
  feta cheese

½ cup (about) whole wheat
  breadcrumbs*

¼ cup grated Asiago or
  Parmesan cheese

*Use brown-rice breadcrumbs for
  a gluten-free option.

MAKE

On lightly sprayed baking sheet, place squash halves, skin up. Bake in 350°F oven until flesh pierces easily with tip of knife, 30 to 40 minutes. Let cool enough to handle. Meanwhile, in large saucepan or skillet, heat oil over medium heat. Sauté shallot until tender. Stir in tomatoes, garlic, olives and basil and cook until warmed through. Scoop flesh from squash and transfer to large casserole dish. Toss in tomato mixture and feta to combine. Sprinkle evenly with breadcrumbs and cheese. Return to oven and bake until bubbling, about 20 minutes.

Serves 6 to 8.

"All this talk about Squashghetti Bake... can we just have it for supper? I love how it tastes like noodles!"
— Carter, age 5

REAL SALADS & SIDES

Salads and side dishes provide a safe backup when you are trying a new main course — you'll know you've got something healthy on the side that your kids will eat. Salads and sides can also add solid nutrition to an otherwise not-so-perfect meal such as takeout pizza. It's key to have a few quick, healthy sides that you can make with confidence, and know your family will enjoy, and to have the ingredients on hand for a no-fuss mealtime boost. This chapter will get you started!

No More
INSTANT POTATOES!

Throw out the instant mashed potatoes because cauliflower is a great source of fibre, vitamin C and folate, and contains sulforaphane (which may help to prevent cancer) as well as indole-3-carbinol or I3C (which may help to inhibit the growth of cancer cells).

CREAMY MASHED CAULIFLOWER instead!

GATHER

1 head cauliflower, broken into florets

1 clove garlic, crushed

$1\frac{1}{3}$ cup plain Greek yogourt

¼ teaspoon salt

¼ teaspoon pepper

Chopped fresh chives (optional)

MAKE

In large pot, cover cauliflower with water and bring to a boil. Cook until tender and drain. In food processor or blender, combine cauliflower, garlic, yogourt, salt and pepper and blend until smooth. Garnish with chives, if desired.

Serves 6.

No More
DELI COLESLAW!

If you've got a food processor fitted with a grater attachment, making coleslaw is as easy as buying it in a container. Alternatively, you can buy undressed preshredded slaw mixture (in the produce aisle) and dress it yourself. Try mixing different colours and textures of cabbage and experiment with adding non-traditional veggies, such as broccoli stems or raw sweet potato, into the mix. My kids love this salad, and adults think it's yum, too.

ASIAN SLAW *instead!*

GATHER

3 carrots, shredded

3 green onions, minced

1 large apple (unpeeled if organic), diced

4 cups shredded cabbage

½ cup toasted broken walnuts (optional)

2 tablespoons black or white sesame seeds (optional)

¼ cup flaxseed oil or extra-virgin olive oil

3 tablespoons apple cider vinegar

1½ teaspoons liquid honey

½ teaspoon toasted sesame oil

½ teaspoon salt

¼ teaspoon pepper

MAKE

In large bowl, toss together carrots, green onions, apple, cabbage and walnuts and sesame seeds, if desired. In small bowl, whisk together flaxseed or olive oil, vinegar, honey, sesame oil, salt and pepper. Toss into carrot and cabbage mixture to coat.

Serves 6 to 8.

No More
BAGGED SALAD!

You can use any dark greens for this recipe. Since most dark leafy greens significantly shrink when cooked, this is a great way to pack a lot into a small serving, which can be a lot less overwhelming to kids (and spouses) who may be anti-green.

SIMPLE SESAME GREENS *instead!*

GATHER

2 cloves garlic, crushed

1 tablespoon extra-virgin olive oil

8 cups coarsely chopped kale,
   spinach, chard or other greens

1 tablespoon low-sodium soy sauce

½ teaspoon toasted sesame oil

½ teaspoon liquid honey or
   maple syrup

MAKE

In large skillet or wok, heat garlic and olive oil. Add greens and stir-fry until bright green and starting to wilt, about 3 minutes. In glass measure, whisk together soy sauce, sesame oil and honey. Toss into greens mixture to coat.

Tip: To remove stems from dark leafy greens other than spinach, hold stalk in one hand, then, with the other hand, strip leaf up along stem (or, with sharp knife, slice off leaf up each side of stalk). Tear or chop big leaves into bite-size pieces, transfer to large bowl of water and rinse. Cook just before serving; they are best fresh.

Serves 4.

Best way to clean out your pantry? This recipe!

When creating this recipe, I used the veggies I had on hand, but you could substitute just about anything in here and it would taste just as yummy, so use your imagination.

RAINBOW SALAD instead!

GATHER

8 to 10 small beets (or 4 to 5 large), peeled and cubed

8 to 10 cloves garlic, halved lengthwise

1 to 2 large carrots, peeled and cubed

1 small yam or sweet potato, peeled and cubed

1 onion or large shallot, chopped

2 cups Brussels sprouts, halved lengthwise and stems trimmed

2 tablespoons melted coconut oil

2 cups kale, stems removed, finely chopped

3 tablespoons balsamic vinegar

Salt and pepper to taste

½ cup toasted chopped pecans (optional)

MAKE

In roasting pan or 9- x 11-inch baking dish, toss together beets, garlic, carrots, yam, onion and Brussels sprouts. Toss melted coconut oil with vegetables in pan to coat. Bake in 450°F oven, stirring occasionally, for 35 to 40 minutes until tender.

Remove from oven, top with kale. Return to oven and bake, stirring once halfway through, for 10 minutes.

Toss in vinegar to coat. Add salt and pepper to taste. Sprinkle with pecans.

Serves 6 to 8.

VEGAN OPTION

DAIRY-FREE OPTION

GLUTEN-FREE OPTION

NUT-FREE OPTION

This kale salad is crazy good, and it's crazy how much my eight-year-old son likes it. He actually sat down one day before hockey and said "Awesome!" when he saw it in the bowl. Crazy, right? You know this is about as good as it gets.

Kale is easy to include in cooked dishes, but it's trickier to make raw kale really tasty. The secret? Marinate the kale overnight to soften it up. This salad takes just minutes to assemble, then it simply sits in the fridge marinating until you are ready to garnish and serve. It also keeps well in the refrigerator for a few days, so you can include it in lunches for several days.

KRAZY KALE SALAD instead!

GATHER

1 large bunch kale, stems removed, coarsely chopped

¼ cup finely chopped shallot

3 tablespoons apple cider vinegar

1 tablespoon extra-virgin olive oil

1 teaspoon liquid honey

½ teaspoon sea salt

¼ teaspoon pepper

⅓ cup chopped walnuts (optional)

¼ cup grated Asiago or Parmesan cheese (optional)

MAKE

Place kale in lidded bowl or container. In small bowl, whisk together shallots, vinegar, oil, honey, salt and pepper. Toss into kale, cover and refrigerate, tossing occasionally, for at least 8 hours. Toss in walnuts and cheese, if desired, just before serving.

Serves 8 to 10.

No More
FROZEN FRIES!

Kids love fries but sweet potatoes provide more beta carotene (a precursor of vitamin A) and soluble fibre than regular white potatoes, so include them in your family's diet. If you've tried sweet-potato fries before and they've been a bit soggy, don't worry. I tried various permutations and variations, chasing the elusive crispy baked fries, and I believe I've finally cracked the code. Even if you don't hit the ultra-crispy jackpot, these fries are always ultra-yummy and your family will love them. So what do you have to lose?

SWEET POTATO FRIES instead!

GATHER

2 unpeeled large sweet potatoes, scrubbed

2 tablespoons whole wheat flour*

¼ teaspoon paprika

⅛ teaspoon sea salt

2 teaspoons coconut oil

1 clove garlic, crushed

*For a gluten-free alternative, use brown-rice flour.

MAKE

Place 2 baking sheets inside a 425°F oven to preheat.

Cut potatoes into 2- to 3-inch "fries," about ½ inch thick, trimming off any thin, pointy tips.

In plastic bag, combine flour, paprika and salt. Add sweet potatoes, blow a little air into bag, gather and shake well to coat fries with flour mixture.

Remove baking sheets from oven, then spread single layer of fries over top (don't overcrowd or they won't crisp up).

Melt coconut oil and then combine with garlic in a small bowl. Drizzle over fries.

Bake, switching pans between oven racks and turning fries once after 20 minutes, until browned and crisp, about 35 minutes. Serve with Hurry Up Curry Mayo (page 98) for dipping.

Tip: To improve the chances for crispy fries, immerse cut fries in cold water and let soak for an hour, then spin dry in a salad spinner, before coating and baking.

Serves 6.

Superfoods for Superkids: Truly Sweet Sweet Potatoes

A pretty easy sell, sweet potatoes can be prepared any way kids like to eat regular potatoes: baked, roasted or mashed, or in soups and stews. They can even be sweetened with maple syrup and cinnamon to satisfy a sweet tooth.

Sweet potatoes are loaded with beta carotene (short for "supersight," in kid-speak), potassium, iron (short for "super-strength," in kid-speak), fibre and vitamins E and B6.

Easiest way to get your kids to admit they like sweet potatoes? Try the Jack's Snack (Sweet Potato Snackin' Cake) on page 117. Don't forget to tell them the secret ingredient (sweet potato) after they ask for seconds!

No More
INSTANT POTATOES!

This healthy vegan version of scalloped potatoes is made with real ingredients and is just as yummy as the classic dish. My son had begged me to buy the prepackaged scalloped potatoes he has had at his grandma's a few times, so I had to come up with a real-food version. This one earned a thumbs-up from everyone at the table.

HEALTHY SCALLOPED POTATOES *instead!*

GATHER

⅓ cup whole wheat or spelt flour

1 teaspoon salt

¾ teaspoon pepper

6 potatoes (preferably organic),
   peeled and thinly sliced

1 onion, finely chopped

3 tablespoons extra-virgin olive oil

1 clove garlic, crushed

2 cups unsweetened almond milk

¼ cup nutritional yeast

Paprika

MAKE

In small bowl, whisk together flour, salt and pepper.

In lightly sprayed 9-inch baking pan, arrange one-third of the potatoes in single layer, top with one-third of the onion, drizzle with 1 tablespoon of the oil, then sprinkle with half of the flour mixture. Repeat. Top with remaining potatoes, onion and oil.

In bowl, stir together garlic, milk and yeast. Slowly pour into pan over potato mixture. Sprinkle with paprika.

Bake in 350°F oven until potatoes are tender and sauce has thickened, 1½ to 2 hours.

Serves 10.

No More
PASTA SALAD MIX!

VEGETARIAN OPTION

GLUTEN-FREE OPTION

NUT-FREE OPTION

This great summertime salad is perfect for a big family barbecue, potluck pool party or a Sunday dinner with leftovers that fill lunch bags all week long. You won't miss boxed pasta salads or unhealthy versions from the deli counter. If you have some fresh herbs growing on your windowsill or deck, this is the perfect last-minute recipe. Just sprinkle them over any veggies you happen to have on hand, then roast. You can serve this warm or at room temperature.

ROASTED VEGGIE PENNE SALAD instead!

GATHER

2 boxes (454 g each) whole wheat penne*

10 to 12 baby potatoes, scrubbed and quartered

2 to 3 bell peppers, seeded and cut in 1-inch squares

1 unpeeled zucchini, cut in 1-inch cubes

1 onion, cut in large chunks

1 bunch trimmed asparagus, cut in 1-inch lengths

¾ cup + 1 tablespoon extra-virgin olive oil, divided

5 tablespoons balsamic vinegar, divided

2 cloves garlic

1 cup fresh basil

1 cup parsley

3 tablespoons red wine vinegar

3 tablespoons water

½ cup crumbled light goat or feta cheese

Sea salt and pepper to taste

*For a gluten-free salad, use brown-rice pasta.

MAKE

Cook pasta according to package directions, drain and rinse with cold water. Transfer to large bowl and set aside.

In another large bowl, toss together potatoes, peppers, zucchini, onion, asparagus, 1 tablespoon of the oil, 2 tablespoons of the balsamic vinegar and pinch of salt to coat. Spread over grilling tray. Grill over medium heat, turning occasionally, until potatoes and asparagus are tender, 12 to 15 minutes.

In food processor, combine 3 tablespoons balsamic vinegar, garlic, basil, parsley, red wine vinegar and water and blend until combined. Slowly pour in remaining oil, blending until smooth.

Into pasta, toss potato mixture, dressing and cheese. Season to taste with salt and pepper.

Serves 15.

No More
INSTANT BISCUITS!

In 5 minutes, you can whip up your own 6-ingredient whole-grain biscuits. These healthy tea biscuits are great alongside any soup or stew. Named after my daughter, who loves 'em, these might just become your new staple side dish!

GEORGIA BUNS *instead!*

GATHER

2 cups whole wheat pastry flour

1 tablespoon aluminum-free
   baking powder

¾ teaspoon sea salt

2 tablespoons cold unsalted butter

½ cup grated Parmesan or Asiago
   cheese, or shredded white
   cheddar cheese (optional)

¾ cup unsweetened almond or
   cow's milk

MAKE

In bowl, whisk together flour, baking powder and salt. With pastry blender or 2 knives, cut in butter into pea-size crumbs. Stir in cheese, if desired.

Slowly pour in milk, mixing with metal spoon, until combined and doughy but not wet.

With hands, loosely shape into 8 balls and transfer to nonstick baking sheet.

Bake in 400°F oven until golden, about 15 minutes.

Serves 8.

REAL DIPS & SAUCES

Anyone with a toddler at home knows that dips and sauces can be a parent's best friend. A tasty dip can convince even the pickiest eater to try a new food. Unfortunately, commercial dips and sauces are often full of salt, sugar, hydrogenated oils and numerous unpronounceable ingredients that stretch out their shelf life.

I love dips. If I do say so myself, I'm a bit of a dip ninja. I've included some family favourites in this chapter. They are all straightforward and quick, so get your dip ninja on.

"Mmmmm, hummus is yummy, more please!"

— Tyler, age 2½

Why Beancounters Love Beans: A Cheap and Healthy Alternative!

Canned beans are an inexpensive alternative to animal protein, but they're often chock full of sodium, and you may also be concerned about the Bisphenol A (BPA) found in can liners. Both concerns are easy to remedy by cooking dried beans from scratch. It's a lot easier than you might think, and with just a little planning, you can have a freezer full of frozen cooked beans ready to use in any recipe, leaving the sodium and BPA behind.

No More
CHIP DIP!

These dips are so easy you won't need chip dip anymore! You can whip them up during a commercial break. They are all delicious with raw veggies, Asiago and Garlic Pita Chips (page 109) or as a condiment on a veggie burger.

ROASTED RED PEPPER
AND CHICKPEA DIP *instead!*

GATHER

1 clove garlic, crushed

1 cup chickpeas

½ cup drained roasted red peppers

¼ cup light (12% mf) goat or light feta cheese

¼ cup plain Greek yogourt

½ teaspoon Dijon mustard

½ teaspoon balsamic vinegar

1 tablespoon extra-virgin olive oil

MAKE

In food processor, combine garlic, chickpeas, red peppers, cheese, yogourt, mustard and vinegar and blend until smooth. Slowly pour in oil, blending until combined.

Serves 7.

We call this Double Dip because everyone always goes back for more. A great change from hummus, it has no garlic — just a lovely lemony pepper flavour. It's excellent on crostini, in a sandwich or as a dip with raw veggies. My kids really like it, and I pack it in their lunchboxes with veggies and whole-grain crackers or pita wedges.

DOUBLE DIP instead!

GATHER

3 cups fresh-cooked white beans (or canned), rinsed and drained

5 tablespoons water, divided

Juice of 1 lemon

1 tablespoon fresh rosemary (or 1 teaspoon dried)

1½ teaspoons sea salt

1 teaspoon dried parsley (or 1 to 2 tablespoons fresh)

½ teaspoon pepper

¼ teaspoon nutmeg

¼ teaspoon dried thyme

¼ cup extra-virgin olive oil

MAKE

In food processor, combine beans, 4 tablespoons of the water, the lemon juice, rosemary, salt, parsley, pepper, nutmeg and thyme and pulse several times, until chunky. Slowly pour in oil, blending and adding more water only if mixture is very dry and not combining completely, until smooth (the consistency of hummus).

Serves 12.

YUMMUS HUMMUS instead!

GATHER

¼ cup (about) water

Juice of 1 lemon

1 clove garlic, crushed

1 can (19 oz) chickpeas (or 2 cups home-cooked chickpeas), rinsed and drained

⅓ cup tahini

2 teaspoons ground cumin

1 teaspoon salt

MAKE

In food processor, combine all ingredients and blend, adding more water if necessary for desired consistency, until smooth.

Tip: Spoon hummus or any bean dip into ice cube trays, then cover and freeze. You can pop a cube into a small container in the morning and it will be defrosted by lunchtime.

Serves 7.

This is a simple, no-fail hummus, and you can adjust any of the ingredients up or down, to taste. Love garlic? Add another clove. Lemon? Throw in a little grated zest along with the juice. Drained, roasted red peppers from a jar also make a yummy addition. My family also loves this as a sandwich spread — it's especially delicious with roasted veggies.

This yummy hybrid mixes avocado and edamame to produce a creamy green dip packed with healthy fat, protein and vitamins.

If you prefer a chunkier guacamole, use a fork to coarsely mash together the beans and avocado, then mix in the remaining ingredients by hand. If you like it smooth, follow these simple directions. Serve with tortilla or pita chips and raw veggies.

HOLY "GUADAMAME" instead!

GATHER

Juice of 1 lemon

1 avocado, peeled and pitted

1 clove garlic, crushed

1 cup cooked organic edamame, shelled

¼ cup plain Greek yogourt

¼ cup onion, minced

¼ teaspoon ground cumin

¼ teaspoon chili powder

¼ teaspoon sea salt

MAKE

In food processor, combine all ingredients and blend until smooth.

Serves 8.

Avocados Anonymous

I am an avocado addict. When I'm in Mexico, I eat my weight in guacamole. To make myself feel better about my habit, I remember these lovely avocado facts: Avocados contain all 18 essential amino acids (unusual in the plant world); avocados are a great source of both antioxidants and omega-3 anti-inflammatory fatty acids, and; avocado consumption boosts good cholesterol (HDL) levels.

A perfectly ripe avocado should have no dents and feel just slightly soft when gently squeezed. To keep guacamole from browning, put one of the avocado pits back into the bowl until it's time to serve the dip or pour a few drops of milk on the dip, then cover and store it in the fridge until serving. Just stir the milk in before serving if that's the method you used. Who knew? Now, if only I could figure out how to make those unbelievably delicious authentic Mexican tortilla chips healthy...

VEGETARIAN
OPTION

GLUTEN-FREE
OPTION

NUT-FREE
OPTION

Yum. Yum. Yum. Enjoy this quick and easy caramel dip with delicious local fall apples. You'll never for back for the store-bought caramel again!

The Greek yogourt provides some protein and the unsulphured molasses is a source of calcium, magnesium and potassium, as well as iron, vitamin B6, selenium and copper. Unsulphured molasses provides far more nutrition than granulated sugar (which yields calories and carbs, but nothing else, making it non-food in my book). Whip up this treat in 5 minutes and enjoy. It's also school-lunch safe (just make sure you keep it cool)!

LITTLE DIPPER instead!

GATHER

¼ cup plain Greek yogourt

1½ teaspoons real maple syrup

1 teaspoon unsulphured molasses

½ teaspoon vanilla

¼ teaspoon cinnamon

Apples, sliced

MAKE

In small bowl, with spoon, blend yogourt, maple syrup, molasses, vanilla and cinnamon. Serve with apples.

Serves 7.

Here's another simple dip for fruit. If you use plain Greek yogourt, you will get a thicker dip with a much higher protein content than if you use regular plain yogourt. If using regular yogourt, check the label and choose a brand that contains 18 to 20 grams of protein per serving.

SWEET FRUIT DIP *instead!*

GATHER

1 cup plain Greek yogourt

1½ tablespoons liquid honey or maple syrup

1 to 2 teaspoons grated orange zest (optional)

1 teaspoon vanilla extract

½ teaspoon cinnamon

Sliced fruit, banana chunks or fruit kebabs

MAKE

In small bowl, with fork, blend yogourt, honey, orange zest (if desired), vanilla and cinnamon. Serve with fruit.

Serves 6.

This delicious dressing packs a healthy hit of omega-3 thanks to the flaxseed oil. It's great in wraps, as a dip or on salads. This dressing will thicken when it's chilled.

LESS IS MORE CAESAR *instead!*

VEGETARIAN OPTION

GLUTEN-FREE OPTION

NUT-FREE OPTION

GATHER

1 clove garlic, crushed

1 cup extra-soft or soft silken tofu

¼ cup grated Parmesan cheese

1 tablespoon Dijon mustard

1 tablespoon lemon juice

1½ teaspoons white wine vinegar

Pinch sea salt

Pinch pepper

2 tablespoons flaxseed oil

MAKE

In food processor, combine garlic, tofu, Parmesan, mustard, lemon juice, vinegar, salt and pepper and blend. Slowly pour in oil, blending until smooth. (Use immediately or transfer to airtight container and refrigerate.)

Serves 12.

Serve this savoury dip/dressing with pita chips, whole-grain crackers or raw veggies. It's also great with falafels or as a topping for veggie burgers. With only four ingredients, it takes less than 5 minutes to make. For a thicker dip, mix it by hand; for a smoother, more pourable sauce, blend the ingredients. When mixing this for young children, I only use half a clove of garlic.

TASTY TZATZIKI *instead!*

GATHER

1 cucumber, peeled and seeded

1 clove garlic, minced

1 cup plain Greek yogourt

1/3 cup finely chopped mint
   (or 2 to 3 teaspoons dried)
   or 2 to 3 tablespoons chopped
   fresh dill

MAKE

Against large holes in box grater, grate cucumber into colander. Over sink, squeeze cucumber against colander to press out excess liquid. Transfer to bowl.

   Stir in remaining ingredients to combine.

Tip: If your kids want to help, let them squeeze handfuls of grated cucumber over the sink to squish out the excess liquid.

Serves 8.

VEGETARIAN OPTION

GLUTEN-FREE OPTION

NUT-FREE OPTION

Here's another good reason to keep plain Greek yogourt on hand. This dip is perfect with Coconut Pecan Crusted Nuggets (page 63). It's also nice with whole-grain pretzels or crackers.

BUSY BEE DIP *instead!*

GATHER

1/3 cup plain Greek yogourt

1 tablespoon + 1 teaspoon liquid
  honey

1 teaspoon prepared or Dijon
  mustard

MAKE

In bowl, whisk together all ingredients to blend.

Serves 4.

I always have plain Greek yogourt in my fridge for last-minute dip emergencies. This is my go-to dip for Sweet Potato Fries (page 84). It's guilt-free, delicious comfort food.

HURRY UP CURRY MAYO *instead!*

GATHER

1/3 cup plain Greek yogourt

1/2 teaspoon mild curry powder

1/4 teaspoon lemon or lime juice

MAKE

In bowl, whisk together all ingredients to blend.

Serves 4.

REAL SNACKS & TREATS

The best family snacks combine proteins, healthy fats and complex carbohydrates. This winning combo provides longer-lasting energy and eliminates the sugar highs and lows of refined, processed treats. We've all witnessed the nasty aftermath of that cycle!

Most processed, prepackaged snacks are high in sugar and low in fibre, a combination that quickly spikes blood sugar, but gives no lasting energy. Often these snacks also contain nasty ingredients such as high-fructose corn syrup, high-sodium hydrogenated oils, and artificial colours and flavours.

This chapter offers healthy, balanced alternatives for many of the popular commercial snacks and treats familiar to Canadian families. Many of these recipes are nut-free or can be easily adapted to allow your kids to take them to school and other activities. Most can be made in bulk in advance and frozen for convenience, and they are all delicious!

No More
GOLDFISH!

I admit, I was hesitant to propose an alternative recipe for goldfish crackers because I honestly couldn't see any busy parent having the time to make a batch of tiny crackers. But, because we feed the processed version of these crackers to our toddlers like candy, and because they are made with white flour and sugar, I gave a healthier recipe (with 100 per cent whole wheat) a shot. Turns out, my kids not only love my version, but you can whip up a batch in 25 minutes. Roll out the dough, quickly cut the crackers with a miniature-fish cookie cutter, then pop them into the oven.

What?! You don't own a little fishy cookie cutter? Me neither. You can order them online, but I've also included my DIY workaround in the sidebar, if you feel like channelling Martha Stewart! Even easier? Cut your dough into little squares and call them cheese nips!

FREE-RANGE GOLDFISH
CHEESE CRACKERS instead!

GATHER

1 cup large-flake rolled oats

½ cup whole wheat pastry flour

⅓ cup ground flaxseed

¼ teaspoon salt

1 cup shredded white old cheddar
   cheese*

⅓ cup cold water

¼ cup melted coconut oil

1 teaspoon prepared mustard

1 tablespoon sesame seeds
   (optional)

*For dairy-free, more savoury
   crackers, replace cheddar with
   3 tablespoons nutritional yeast
   and 1 teaspoon onion powder,
   then increase salt to ½ teaspoon.

MAKE

In food processor, pulse oats to a coarse flour. Add flour, flaxseed and salt and blend until combined. Add cheddar, water, melted oil and mustard and blend until dough forms ball.

On lightly floured surface, flatten ball into disc. Roll out as thinly as possible. Sprinkle with sesame seeds, if desired, then roll over seeds to adhere. With cookie cutter, cut out crackers and transfer to parchment paper–lined baking sheets.

Bake one sheet at a time in 350°F oven until bottoms are just lightly golden, about 15 minutes.

Serves 15.

"More please."

– Noah, age 2

Mmmm

Make Your Own Mini Fish Cookie Cutter!

To make your own cheap-and-cheerful fish cookie cutter, cut a 1-inch strip from waxed cardboard milk container or Tetra Pak. Clean thoroughly and dry. Shape strip into small fish, taping strip ends together at top edges of tail — et voilà! Instant cookie cutter!

No More
STORE-BOUGHT
COOKIES!

This recipe has been evolving for years in my kitchen, getting a little healthier each time. Store-bought cookies often contain artificial flavours, hydrogenated fats and high-fructose corn syrup, but not these nut-free, lunchbox-friendly treats!

CINNAMON CARROT COOKIES instead!

GATHER

1 ripe banana, mashed

½ cup softened coconut oil

½ cup packed brown sugar

1 large egg

1 teaspoon vanilla extract

1 cup finely grated carrots

½ cup finely grated zucchini

1¾ cups whole wheat flour

½ cup all-purpose flour

¼ cup flax meal

2 teaspoons cinnamon

1½ teaspoons aluminum-free
   baking powder

½ teaspoon nutmeg

½ teaspoon salt

1 cup raisins

MAKE

In large bowl, with electric mixer, beat together banana, oil and sugar until light and fluffy. Beat in egg and vanilla to blend. Stir in carrots and zucchini.

In another bowl, whisk together whole wheat flour, all-purpose flour, flax meal, cinnamon, baking powder, nutmeg and salt. One-third at a time, add to banana mixture, stirring to combine after each addition. Stir in raisins.

With hands, roll into about 32 balls and transfer to two un-greased baking sheets. With moistened fork, slightly flatten.

Bake, one sheet at a time, in 350°F oven until golden brown, about 14 minutes per batch.

Makes 32 cookies.

"Yummy! Can we make some more?"
— Ella, age 7

No More
FRUIT ROLLUPS!

Packaged fruit snacks often contain added sugars and artificial colours — things we'd rather not feed our kids. Are you thinking: "Nope. Not doin' it. Don't have time for that"? That's what I used to think, but, turns out, a big batch of these takes only 10 minutes to prepare. The downside? It takes 7 to 10 hours to cook. The upside? You can repaint the bathroom, spring clean the house or get a good night's sleep while it's cooking. Once it's in the oven, it's completely hands-free!

PEAR, APPLE AND
CINNAMON FRUIT ROLLS *instead!*

GATHER

4 cups chopped unpeeled organic
   pears (about 4 large)

4 cups chopped unpeeled organic
   apples (about 4 large)

¼ cup lemon juice

2 tablespoons liquid honey

1 teaspoon vanilla extract

½ teaspoon cinnamon

MAKE

In food processor, combine all ingredients and blend until smooth.

Spread half of the mixture over each of two parchment paper–lined baking sheets, then shake each sheet back and forth to even out mixture.

Dry in 170°F oven with door left open a crack, until mixture is leathery, tight and dry to the touch, 7 to 10 hours. Transfer pans to racks and let cool in pans.

Once cool, cut each sheet into 16 one-inch-wide strips, leaving the paper on. Tightly roll each strip, then transfer to an airtight container.

Makes 16 rolls.

No More
POPSICLES!

Hot summer weather always leads to a feast of homemade frozen treats on sticks around my house. Supply can never keep up with demand! Healthy, cheap and easy, chilly treats are a great way to get small children into the kitchen.

You will need a mould (choose BPA-free plastic) or some small disposable cups and some wooden sticks. Then check out these easy recipes and get started. When the moulds are empty, just whip up another batch. I love using Greek yogourt because it's easy to find low-fat or no-fat varieties, and it's very high in protein. Thick and creamy, it's perfect for frozen treats. Spinach, you say? Trust me, its flavour will disappear when it's combined with the fruit and honey, and you'll be the smug one when your kids ask you for more!

BLUEBERRY BANANA POPS *instead!*

GATHER

1 banana

2 cups frozen or fresh blueberries
  or strawberries

2 cups baby spinach

1 cup plain Greek yogourt

1 cup pure apple or orange juice

1 cup water

2 teaspoons liquid honey

1 teaspoon vanilla extract

MAKE

In food processor or blender, combine all ingredients and blend until smooth. Pour into 12 large moulds and freeze until solid, at least 4 hours.

Makes 12 pops.

Oh holy creamy! These are divine. In my childhood, I was a lover of Fudgsicles, but then, as now, anything cold and chocolate was a hit with me. I'm not a big fan of what's also in the commercial brand, in particular, the high-fructose corn syrup. I wanted to come up with a natural alternative and I think I've hit this one out of the park, but you be the judge!

NATURAL FUDGE POPS instead!

GATHER

⅔ cup pitted dates

2 bananas

2 cups coconut milk

4 tablespoons cocoa powder

1 tablespoon liquid honey

1 teaspoon vanilla extract

MAKE

In food processor, pulse dates until finely chopped. Add remaining ingredients and pulse until smooth and blended. Pour into 6 moulds and freeze until solid, at least 4 hours.

Serves 6.

"My two favourite snacks are Natural Fudge Pops and Kalato Chips. They're both so good I don't want to choose."

– Mae, age 8

No More
BITS & BITES!

This is a delicious, healthier version of a commercial party mix like Bits & Bites, without the refined flour, preservatives and MSG — it's made entirely with whole grains and real ingredients. It can be made nut-free for a school-friendly snack and is a guaranteed crowd-pleaser at family gatherings, game nights and holiday parties.

WHOLE-GRAIN SNACK MIX *instead!*

GATHER

1 clove garlic, halved

2 cups whole wheat Os cereal*

2 cups shredded wheat squares
   cereal*

2 cups brown-rice puffed cereal*

½ cup raw sunflower seeds

½ cup raw almonds**

½ cup raw pumpkin seeds

1 clove garlic, crushed

¼ cup melted coconut oil

1 tablespoon sodium-reduced soy
   sauce

½ teaspoon onion powder

1/3 teaspoon Herbamare seasoning
   salt*

*Available in the natural food
   section of grocery stores or health
   food stores.

**For a school-friendly, nut-free
   treat, eliminate almonds and add
   ½ cup more seeds of your choice.

MAKE

With clove garlic halves, rub all over inside large roasting pan, then add Os cereal, squares cereal, puffed cereal, sunflower seeds, almonds and pumpkin seeds and toss to combine. In glass measure, stir together crushed garlic, oil, soy sauce, onion powder and seasoning salt. Drizzle over mixture in pan and, with hands, toss to coat.

Bake in 250°F oven, stirring every 15 minutes, for 45 minutes. Let cool. Transfer to airtight container. They'll keep for a few days if you can stop your family from eating them!

Serves 10.

VEGAN
OPTION

DAIRY-FREE
OPTION

GLUTEN-FREE
OPTION

NUT-FREE
OPTION

No More
POTATO CHIPS!

Here are some favourite crunchy alternatives to high-fat high-sodium potato chips. On family movie nights, my kids devour a bowlful of healthier options without blinking. Thanks to the kale, my children christened these Kalato Chips. Believe me, these are great! Give them a chance. Crazily simple to make, these are so tasty that they won't last long. Oh, come on ... just try them. They take 25 minutes to make and only have three ingredients!

KALATO CHIPS instead!

GATHER

1 large bunch fresh kale,
    destemmed and shredded in large
    pieces and patted or spun dry
1 tablespoon extra-virgin olive oil
Sea salt

MAKE

In bowl, toss together kale and oil to coat. In single layer, transfer to two nonstick (or parchment paper–lined) baking sheets. Very lightly sprinkle with salt.

Bake in 325°F oven until crisp (watch carefully and do not let brown), 10 to 15 minutes. You may need to make more than one batch if your kale bunch is large. The key is to spread out the kale so that it cooks evenly.

Tip: Keep some olive oil in a pump mister to speed things up. For this recipe, use it for spraying the kale leaves, instead of tossing with oil (you will use less oil).

Serves 4 to 6.

"Who knew leaves could taste so good?"

— Jaiden, age 12

ASIAGO AND GARLIC PITA CHIPS *instead!*

GATHER

3 small whole wheat pitas

Olive oil in pump mister

2 tablespoons grated Asiago cheese

¼ teaspoon garlic powder

MAKE

Halve each pita, then cut into 6 triangles. In single layer, transfer to nonstick baking sheet. Lightly spray with oil and sprinkle with Asiago and garlic powder.

Bake in 325°F oven for 7 minutes. With tongs, gently turn over and bake until golden and crisp, 2 to 3 minutes. Let cool.

Serves 4.

VEGETARIAN OPTION

NUT-FREE OPTION

High in protein and fibre, these are a tasty alternative to potato chips, surprisingly satisfying and crunchy as a snack. You can also use them as a salad topper or add them to savoury homemade trail mix.

VEGAN
OPTION

DAIRY-FREE
OPTION

GLUTEN-FREE
OPTION

NUT-FREE
OPTION

CRUNCHY CHICKPEAS *instead!*

GATHER

1 can (14 oz) chickpeas, rinsed, drained and patted dry

$1/3$ teaspoon extra-virgin olive oil

$1/4$ teaspoon garlic powder

Pinch sea salt

MAKE

On nonstick baking sheet, spread chickpeas.

Bake in 325°F oven, shaking pan occasionally and watching carefully to prevent burning, until golden and crunchy (test one to ensure it is crisp in centre), about 65 minutes. Transfer to heat-proof bowl. Toss in oil, garlic powder and salt to coat.

Serves 6.

"Crunchy. Salty. Yummy."

– Dahlia, age 6

No More
ROASTED, SALTED NUTS!

VEGETARIAN OPTION

DAIRY-FREE OPTION

GLUTEN-FREE OPTION

Did you know that if nuts are roasted at too high a temperature, they can become unhealthy? At very high heat, the good fats in almonds, for example, can oxidize and become rancid. To avoid this, I recommend buying raw nuts and roasting them at home. That way, you control the temperature to ensure their goodness is preserved. You can also control the flavour — salty or sweet, you choose!

SIMPLE ROASTED ALMONDS instead!

GATHER

2 cups natural almonds

3 tablespoons soy sauce*

*I like Bragg's Soy Seasoning because it's gluten-free and lower in sodium than many alternatives. It is available in natural food aisles at grocery stores or at health food stores.

MAKE

In large bowl, toss together almonds and soy sauce to coat. Transfer to nonstick baking sheet.

Bake in 170°F oven, stirring occasionally, until liquid has been absorbed, about 1 hour 15 minutes. Let cool in pan on rack (almonds become crunchy as they cool). Transfer to airtight container.

Serves 8.

"Yum! I like how these almonds are super crunchy and salty!"
— Jake, age 7

MAPLE-SPICED ALMONDS *instead!*

VEGAN OPTION

DAIRY-FREE OPTION

GLUTEN-FREE OPTION

GATHER

3 tablespoons maple syrup

2 tablespoons pumpkin pie spice

1 tablespoon melted coconut oil

3 cups natural almonds

MAKE

In large bowl, whisk together maple syrup, spice and oil to blend. Toss in almonds to coat. Transfer to parchment paper–lined baking sheet.

Bake in 170°F oven until dry and starting to brown, about 1 hour 45 minutes.

Let cool in pan on rack (almonds become crunchy as they cool). Separating if necessary, transfer to airtight container.

Serves 12.

Superfoods for Superkids!

If no one in your household has a nut allergy, almonds are an excellent food. They are naturally high in antioxidants, healthy monounsaturated fat, protein and many minerals, including manganese, calcium and magnesium. Portable and versatile, they're a great snack, anytime. Technically a seed, almonds usually get lumped into the nut category. Buy them raw, then roast them yourself to control the roasting temperature and the quality of any extra ingredients! Store them in an airtight container in the fridge or freezer, to ensure freshness and keep their good oils stable and healthy. Roasting nuts is an easy way to get kids involved in the kitchen, so why not give one of my recipes a try?

No More
QUAKER BARS!

No more junky granola bars. This straightforward, nut-free recipe has been a hit with everyone in my family, and contains all-natural, nutrient-dense ingredients. The original recipe first appeared online, with my recipe-sharing group. We have all modified it in different ways, but everyone agrees, these are delicious! I removed all of the refined sugar from the original recipe, making this an energy boost you can really feel good about. These little 2-bites make great snacks for active kids, and the large batch leaves some leftovers for the freezer.

2-BITE GRANOLA BARS instead!

GATHER

1 cup pitted dates

1 bar (100 g) dark chocolate (80% or more cocoa solids), coarsely chopped

2½ cups large-flake rolled oats

2 cups whole wheat or spelt flour

1 cup unsalted sunflower seeds

1 cup raisins, unsweetened cranberries or chopped dried fruit

½ cup raw unsalted pumpkin seeds

½ cup unsweetened shredded coconut

¼ cup sesame seeds

¼ cup ground flaxseed

1 tablespoon + 1 teaspoon cinnamon

1 teaspoon sea salt

¼ cup water

¼ cup unsulphured molasses

1 teaspoon vanilla extract

½ cup + 1 teaspoon melted coconut oil

1 cup unsweetened almond or cow's milk

MAKE

In bowl, immerse dates in water, let soak for 10 minutes.

In large bowl, toss together chocolate, oats, flour, sunflower seeds, raisins, pumpkin seeds, coconut, sesame seeds, flaxseed, cinnamon and salt.

Drain dates, pat dry and transfer to food processor. Purée until smooth. Add water, molasses, vanilla, oil and milk and blend until smooth. Add to chocolate mixture. With hands, toss to coat and combine.

Spoon by heaping tablespoonfuls onto parchment paper–lined baking sheets (about 12 per sheet). With fork, lightly flatten.

One baking sheet at a time on top rack, bake in 350°F oven, checking bottoms occasionally to prevent burning, for 20 minutes per batch. Let cool in pans on racks.

Makes about 45 bars.

"I love to have these in my lunch every day! I like how there's lots of chocolate chips!"
— Ben, age 10

This is a simple, delicious, school-safe recipe! Freeze half of the batch and you will have enough recess snacks for two weeks!

CHOCOLATE CHIP GRANOLA BARS *instead!*

GATHER

3 cups large-flake rolled oats

1¾ cups whole wheat flour

¾ cup pitted, finely chopped dates*

¾ cup unsweetened shredded coconut

½ cup raw unsalted sunflower or pumpkin seeds

½ cup dark chocolate chips

¼ cup ground flaxseed

1 teaspoon baking soda

1 large egg + 1 large egg white

½ cup unsweetened applesauce

½ cup maple syrup

3 tablespoons unsweetened almond, soy or cow's milk

2 teaspoons vanilla extract

¼ teaspoon salt

*If dates are dry, soak them in hot water for 10 minutes and drain well before chopping.

MAKE

In large bowl, toss together oats, flour, dates, coconut, sunflower seeds, chocolate chips, flaxseed and baking soda. If your chopped dates are really sticky, use your fingers to break them apart and drop the pieces individually into the mix, tossing with dry mixture as you go, to coat them and prevent clumping.

In bowl, with electric mixer, beat together egg and egg white, applesauce, maple syrup, milk, vanilla and salt. Stir into oat mixture to coat and combine. Press into greased 13- x 9-inch baking pan.

Bake in 350°F oven until golden, 22 to 23 minutes. Let cool in pan on rack. Cut into 25 bars. Transfer to airtight container and refrigerate or freeze.

Makes about 25 bars.

"These granola bars taste SOOO good. You can't even taste the applesauce — they taste like chocolate!"

— Declan, age 6½

No More
INSTANT CAKE MIX!

Making a yummy cake from scratch with healthier ingredients is easy if you stock your pantry with the basics and have a simple recipe.

I cannot be alone in the house with this cake (one of us disappears).

The original recipe came from a woman I heard on the radio. She told the story of a favourite war-bride cake that she used to make as a child with her grandmother, and of her delight when she realized, as an adult, that the recipe was — surprisingly — vegan.

It is unbelievably delicious. It makes an amazing birthday cake or excellent cupcakes. It's so moist and sweet it doesn't really need icing. I've taken to partially blending some frozen berries into a thick syrup, instead, and drizzling that on top. Any of the No More Jemima Syrups (pages 26 to 27) in the breakfast chapter make delicious toppings.

CHOCOLATE "WAR-BRIDE" CAKE OR CUPCAKES instead!

GATHER

1 cup all-purpose flour

1¾ cups whole wheat pastry flour

1½ cups granulated sugar

6 tablespoons cocoa powder

2 teaspoons aluminum-free baking powder

2 teaspoons baking soda

1 teaspoon salt

1 ripe banana, mashed

⅓ cup melted coconut oil

2 tablespoons apple cider vinegar

2 teaspoons vanilla extract

2 cups warm water

MAKE

In bowl, whisk together all-purpose flour, whole wheat flour, sugar, cocoa, baking powder, baking soda and salt.

In small bowl, with fork, mash banana, then stir in melted oil. In flour mixture, form three wells. Pour vinegar into one and vanilla into second well. Spoon banana mixture into third well. Pour water over top and, with wooden spoon, stir together to combine. Scrape into greased 13- x 9-inch baking pan (or spoon into 22 greased muffin tins for cupcakes).

Bake in 350°F oven until toothpick inserted in centre comes out clean, 30 to 35 minutes, or 20 to 25 minutes for cupcakes.

Makes 20 to 22 servings.

My nephew Jack, a highly selective eater, ate two back-to-back servings of this snacking cake at our house one morning. Surprisingly yummy, it's a naturally sweetened, high-fibre, nutrient-dense cake that you can feel good about serving anytime. Really more of a muffin in a pan, it's a great recess snack or a terrific side to a bowl of natural yogourt and fruit at breakfast.

JACK'S SNACK (SWEET POTATO SNACKIN' CAKE) *instead!*

VEGETARIAN OPTION

DAIRY-FREE OPTION

NUT-FREE OPTION

FREEZER-FRIENDLY

GATHER

¾ cup whole wheat flour

½ cup unbleached all-purpose flour

¼ cup ground flaxseed

¼ cup oat bran

1 tablespoon aluminum-free baking powder

1½ teaspoons cinnamon

½ teaspoon salt

½ cup extra-virgin olive oil

¼ cup liquid honey

1 peeled cooked sweet potato, mashed

1 large egg, lightly beaten

1 ripe banana, mashed

½ cup unsweetened applesauce

1 teaspoon vanilla extract

½ cup dried fruit such as cherries, raisins, cranberries, blueberries, chopped prunes, dates or apricots (or a combination)

¼ cup sunflower seeds

MAKE

In large bowl, toss together whole wheat flour, all-purpose flour, flaxseed, bran, baking powder, cinnamon and salt.

In another large bowl, whisk together oil and honey. Whisk in sweet potato, egg, banana, applesauce and vanilla. One-third at a time, add to flour mixture, stirring to blend after each addition. Stir in fruit and seeds. Scrape into greased 8-inch baking pan, smoothing top.

Bake in centre of 350°F oven until golden and toothpick inserted in centre comes out clean, 30 to 35 minutes. Let cool in pan on rack. Cut into 20 squares.

Tip: To cook sweet potato, pierce with fork and microwave until fork-tender, 5 to 7 minutes. Let cool enough to handle. Remove skin, transfer flesh to small bowl and mash.

Makes 20 squares.

"A million thumbs up!"

— Jack, age 9

No More
MICROWAVE POPCORN!

VEGETARIAN OPTION

DAIRY-FREE OPTION

GLUTEN-FREE OPTION

A whole-grain food, popcorn really can be a healthy treat — it's all in the preparation. To avoid genetically modified organisms (GMOs), choose organic popcorn. Use coconut oil, which withstands the high heat required for popping and adds a wonderful, subtle flavour.

Here's our family's movie-night treat of choice. It's my husband's concoction, so all credit goes to him. If you like, you can set some of it aside, let it cool, then pop it into plastic snack bags for school treats.

DAD'S FAMOUS POPCORN instead!

GATHER

2 tablespoons virgin coconut oil

1 cup organic popcorn kernels

2 tablespoons butter, melted*

1/3 teaspoon Herbamare
     seasoning salt

*For a dairy-free vegan treat,
   replace butter with 2 tablespoons
   nutritional yeast.

MAKE

In large, heavy, lidded pot or Dutch oven, heat oil over medium-high heat. Drop in one or two kernels and replace lid. When they pop, add remaining kernels. Cook, shaking pan continuously, until all kernels have popped. Transfer to large heat-proof bowl.

Drizzle butter over top, shaking popcorn to coat. Sprinkle with seasoning salt.

Serves 8.

No More
POWERBARS!

Surprisingly easy to make at home, these simple, nut-free options contain added protein and lots of natural, complex carbs, along with a little healthy fat.

BLUEBERRY LEMON POWER BARS *instead!*

GATHER

2 cups large-flake rolled oats

1 cup whole wheat flour

½ cup protein powder (without artificial sweeteners or flavours)

½ cup packed brown or granulated sugar

½ cup wheat germ

¼ cup ground flaxseed

1 teaspoon cinnamon

¾ teaspoon salt

Zest and juice of 1 lemon

½ cup unsweetened applesauce

½ cup liquid honey

⅓ cup extra-virgin olive oil

2 teaspoons vanilla extract

1 cup fresh or thawed frozen blueberries

MAKE

In large bowl, stir together oats, flour, protein powder, brown sugar, wheat germ, flaxseed, cinnamon and salt to combine.

In small bowl, stir together lemon zest and juice, applesauce, honey, oil and vanilla to blend. Stir into oat mixture. Stir in blueberries. Scrape into greased 13- x 9-inch baking pan, smoothing top. Bake in 350°F oven until top appears dry, 35 to 40 minutes. Let cool in pan on rack for 5 minutes. Cut into 25 bars.

Makes 25 bars.

"*Two thumbs up!*"
— Autumn, age 10

You can feel good about sending these school-safe and portable snacks in the lunchbox. The added protein powder makes them a satisfying snack with staying power, and the sunflower seed butter provides a source of healthy fat. Crispy brown rice, flaxseed and wheat germ add fibre. You can experiment, making these with almond or peanut butter, instead, but then they won't be school-friendly. You could also add cinnamon, a little natural jam or some chopped dates, or even roll these balls in some unsweetened coconut.

CHOCO BUTTER POWERBALLS instead!

GATHER

¾ cup chocolate-flavoured protein powder

⅔ cup crispy brown-rice cereal

2 tablespoons cocoa powder

2 tablespoons wheat germ*

2 tablespoons ground flaxseed

¼ teaspoon salt

½ cup sunflower seed butter (or other nut butter)

⅓ cup liquid honey

1 tablespoon melted coconut oil

1 teaspoon vanilla extract

*For gluten-free option, replace wheat germ with an additional 2 tablespoons flaxseed.

MAKE

In bowl, toss together protein powder, cereal, cocoa powder, wheat germ, flaxseed and salt.

In another bowl, whisk together sunflower seed butter, honey, oil and vanilla to blend. Stir into protein-powder mixture to coat and combine.

With hands, roll into about 25 balls. Cover and refrigerate (or freeze).

Makes about 25 balls.

"These are my favourite recess snack!"
– Drew, age 5

Protein Powder for Kids?

I'm often asked if it's okay to give protein powder to children. The answer is yes, occasionally — as long as the protein powder is a good-quality clean protein (with no added supplements, artificial sweeteners or colours), and as long as you remember a few things: First, kids don't need as much protein as you might think. Second, the recommended serving size on a container of protein powder is for an adult, and is far more protein than is required by a child in a snack. Given this, I usually recommend you only use protein powder if the rest of the meal or snack doesn't otherwise include any protein: for example, if you are making a smoothie and nothing else. Throw in a scoop or two, then share the smoothie among all of your family members, giving the adults and older children a bigger glass than the younger ones. Occasionally adding protein powder to bars and treats to round out the recipe's balance of complex carbs, protein and healthy fat is also a great idea, as it can provide active kids with a long-lasting source of energy and the protein they need to rebuild damaged muscles and grow stronger.

VEGAN OPTION

DAIRY-FREE OPTION

NUT-FREE OPTION

FREEZER-FRIENDLY

No More
PACKAGED COOKIES!

Sweet, chewy and school-safe, these cookies are made with sunflower seed butter instead of the forbidden peanut butter. Find sunflower seed butter in the natural food section of most grocery stores or at health food stores.

Inside, these cookies turn a dark green when they're baked, so don't be alarmed when you take the first bite. The colour surprise doesn't make them taste bad — they are always a hit with my kids!

SUNBUTTER COOKIES instead!

GATHER

1 cup whole wheat pastry flour

1 cup all-purpose flour

1 teaspoon baking soda

1 teaspoon cinnamon

½ teaspoon sea salt

1 cup sunflower seed butter

¾ cup maple syrup

⅓ cup melted coconut oil

¼ cup unsweetened applesauce

2 teaspoons vanilla extract

MAKE

In large bowl, whisk together pastry flour, all-purpose flour, baking soda, cinnamon and salt.

In another bowl, stir together sunflower seed butter, maple syrup, oil, applesauce and vanilla to blend. One-third at a time, stir into flour mixture to loosely combine after each addition (do not overmix).

By tablespoonfuls, drop onto two nonstick or parchment paper–lined baking sheets. With moistened fork, lightly flatten, creating criss-cross pattern on tops.

Bake, one sheet at a time, in 350°F oven for 11 minutes per batch. Transfer to rack and let cool.

Makes about 30 cookies.

The ingredients may surprise you, but my kids go absolutely crazy for these cookies. They are really good. They are also free of both flour and gluten. My son said these should be called Triple Chocolate Cookies, because that's how good they taste.

You can make them with sunflower seed butter to keep them safe for school lunches, and, if you like, add chocolate chips to make them a little bit decadent!

VEGETARIAN OPTION

DAIRY-FREE OPTION

GLUTEN-FREE OPTION

FREEZER-FRIENDLY

CHEWY FLOURLESS FUDGE COOKIES instead!

GATHER

1 cup pitted dates, coarsely chopped

3 large eggs

1½ cups cooked white beans, rinsed and drained

½ cup natural nut or seed butter (peanut, almond, cashew or sunflower seed)

⅓ cup + 1 tablespoon liquid honey

⅓ cup unsweetened shredded coconut

2 tablespoons cocoa powder

2 tablespoons ground flaxseed

1 tablespoon vanilla extract

1 teaspoon aluminum-free baking powder

½ teaspoon cinnamon

¼ cup chopped walnuts or chocolate chips (optional)

MAKE

In small bowl, immerse dates in water. Let soak for 5 minutes, drain and pat dry.

Transfer dates to food processor. Add eggs, beans, nut or seed butter, honey, coconut, cocoa, flaxseed, vanilla, baking powder and cinnamon and blend until smooth. Stir in walnuts or chocolate chips, if desired.

By spoonfuls, drop onto parchment paper–lined baking sheets (6 per pan).

Bake, one sheet at a time, in 350°F oven for 12 minutes per batch. Transfer to racks and let cool (cookies will firm as they cool). Transfer to airtight container (these can also be frozen, if desired).

Makes about 24 cookies.

"These are the best cookies ever."
– Duncan, age 9

No More
BEAR PAWS!

These are a delicious, natural, higher-fibre alternative to the processed kids' snacks that your children will inevitably start begging for once they start school. And you'll feel like Martha Stewart when you pull them out of the oven!

GINGER PAWS *instead!*

GATHER

1¾ cup whole wheat flour

¼ cup ground flaxseed

2 teaspoons baking soda

1½ teaspoons ground ginger

1 teaspoon cinnamon

1 teaspoon nutmeg

½ teaspoon allspice

¼ teaspoon sea salt

½ cup softened coconut oil

½ cup packed brown sugar

1 tablespoon unsweetened apple-sauce

1 large egg

⅓ cup unsulphured molasses

MAKE

In bowl, whisk together whole wheat flour, flaxseed, baking soda, ginger, cinnamon, nutmeg, allspice and salt.

In large bowl, with electric mixer, beat together oil, brown sugar and applesauce until blended. Beat in egg and molasses until creamy. One-third at a time, add flour mixture, stirring to blend after each addition.

By heaping tablespoons, drop "paws" onto parchment paper–lined baking sheet (6 per pan). Along one edge of each paw, add three small "toes."

Bake, one sheet at a time, in 375°F oven until lightly browned and set but still soft, about 10 minutes per batch. Let cool in pans on racks for about 5 minutes. Transfer to racks and let cool.

Makes 12 to 14 paws.

Easy Freezy!

Freezing is the key to variety in lunches. People are always amazed when I explain how many foods can be frozen. Brown rice, for example, is time-consuming and finicky to prepare. Invest in a rice cooker, cook a large batch of brown rice, let it cool, then freeze it in individual portions and simply reheat for real "minute rice." Cook a large batch of beans from dry, then freeze them in 2-cup portions. When a recipe calls for a can of that bean, just pull a portion out of the freezer. When a recipe calls for only 1 tablespoon of tomato paste, scoop the rest of the can into a container and freeze it! Hummus and other bean dips can be frozen in ice cube trays or in mini-muffin tins, for perfect, one-person portions. I also love the idea of freezing individual portions of soups and stews. For this, you can use small Mason jars (leave a little headspace for expansion), then take out the jar(s) for an overnight defrost. You can also send a lot of lunch items to school or the office frozen, knowing they will defrost enough to prevent brain-freeze but still be chilled by lunchtime: yogourt cups, grapes, kiwi chunks, whole strawberries, and banana chunks can all leave the house frozen.

"I really like these. They're even better than the real ones!"
— Bridget, age 8

Index